MERCENARIES, GUNSLINGERS, AND OUTLAWS

Two Years as a Security Contractor in Iraq

Robert M. Kurtz

CASEMATE
Pennsylvania & Yorkshire

Published in the United States of America and Great Britain in 2025 by
CASEMATE PUBLISHERS
1950 Lawrence Road, Havertown, PA 19083
and
47 Church Street, Barnsley, S70 2AS, UK

Copyright 2025 © Robert M. Kurtz

Hardcover Edition: ISBN 978-1-63624-510-2
Digital Edition: ISBN 978-1-63624-511-9

A CIP record for this book is available from the British Library

All rights reserved. No part of this book may be reproduced or transmitted in any form or by any means, electronic or mechanical including photocopying, recording or by any information storage and retrieval system, without permission from the publisher in writing.

Some material in this book has been previously published by the author in the article, "They Called Us Mercenaries, Gunslingers, and Worse: A Contractor's Story," *Soldier of Fortune*, January 2024.

All images from author's collection unless otherwise credited.

Printed and bound in the United Kingdom by CPI Group (UK) Ltd, Croydon, CR0 4YY

Typeset in India by Lapiz Digital Services, Chennai.

For a complete list of Casemate titles, please contact:

CASEMATE PUBLISHERS (US)
Telephone (610) 853-9131
Fax (610) 853-9146
Email: casemate@casematepublishers.com
www.casematepublishers.com

CASEMATE PUBLISHERS (UK)
Telephone (0)1226 734350
Email: casemate@casemateuk.com
www.casemateuk.com

Contents

Prologue — vii

1 Arriving in Iraq — 1

What is a Private Security Contractor? — 5
2 Private Security Details — 7
3 Convoy Security — 10
4 Security Management and Site Security — 13

We're Not in Kansas Anymore — 15
5 The Souk — 16
6 Baghdad's Best Filipino-Run Chinese Restaurant — 18
7 Welcome to Iraq! — 19
8 Recon by Goat Truck — 21

Colorful Characters — 23
9 An Irishman in Baghdad — 24
10 Dandre and the Terrorists — 26
11 The Legionnaire — 28
12 The Car Theft Ring — 30
13 Travels with Casper — 32
14 A Buddhist in Iraq — 35
15 Pieter, the Beehives, and the Reporter — 37

The Land of Not Quite Right — 39
16 OSHA and Extension Cords — 40
17 How to Change a Tire, Iraqi Style — 42
18 Iraqi Plumbing — 44
19 Keeping the Power Flowing — 46
20 "But you said you wanted the left rear window to work" — 48

21	Do Not Embarrass Me!	49
22	Let's Pretend for a Minute That I Know What I'm Talking About	51
23	There is No EPA in Iraq	53

Just Like the Wild Geese — 55
24	Abandoned	56

Life on the Road — 59
25	On Our Own	61
26	A Deadly Environment	63
27	Not Your Average Road Trip	65
28	A Law unto Ourselves	67
29	Crash!	70
30	Traffic Control Convoy Style	73
31	Escalation of Force	76
32	Big Bada' Boom!	78
33	Bullets Hitting a Car Really Do Make Sparks	80
34	Convoy Escort from Abu Ghraib	82
35	The Nisour Square Massacre	84

Gurkhas — 87
36	Conflict Resolution—Gurkha Style	88
37	"Oh, no, Sir. I'm fine"	90
38	Literal Is as Literal Does	92

Firepower — 95
39	Arming on the Cheap	96
40	AKs for Days	98
41	Submachine Guns	100
42	America's Rifle	102
43	Sidearms	103
44	When You Want Something More	105
45	Oddball Stuff	106

Working with Russians — 107
46	Don't Travel Through Kuwait	108
47	Vodka and a Pet Turkey	110

Downtime — 113
- 48 Training — 114
- 49 Killing Time — 116
- 50 Christmas in Iraq — 118

Sex in the City — 121
- 51 The Boy and the Filipino — 122
- 52 A Little Business on the Side — 124

Peshmerga — 125
- 53 "Captain, captain!" — 126
- 54 Ali Baba! — 128
- 55 Pesh Just Like to Shoot Guns — 130

Improvised Explosive Devices — 133
- 56 The Road to Haditha Dam — 135
- 57 The Wreck, the Wedding, and the Marine — 136
- 58 The Convoy — 138
- 59 Death from Above — 140
- 60 Arty Rounds on Haifa Street — 142
- 61 Explosively Formed Penetrators — 144

Working with Expats — 147
- 62 Vacation with the Family, or One of Them Anyway — 148
- 63 Demon Rum in the Green Zone — 150
- 64 A Difference in Perspective — 153

Exploring — 157
- 65 Palaces and Playhouses — 158
- 66 Monuments and Museums — 160
- 67 Radwaniyah — 162

Locals — 165
- 68 The Case Against Making Threats — 167
- 69 Poverty — 169
- 70 Sunnis and Shi'ites — 171
- 71 A Sunni in Shi'ite Country — 173
- 72 Street Kids — 174

73	Alia and Ali	175
74	Litigation Iraqi Style	177
75	Ibrahim and the City of Ur	179
76	Working with Local Sheiks	181

Iraqi Insecurity Forces — 183
77	A Force Divided	185
78	They Don't Let Me Torture People Anymore	187
79	Extortion and Police Commando Escorts	189
80	Um Qasr Checkpoint	192
81	Goodbye to Nasiriyah	195

Losses — 199
82	Archie Gets His Nose Shot Off	200
83	The Trials of Job	201
84	Yam	202
85	The Cost of a Ringtone	204
86	A Tale of Three Contractors	206
87	Need a Little Help Here	208
88	Body Armor Works	211

Epilogue — 213

Prologue

They say you remember your life in more detail as you get older. I've found this to be true, especially in the introspective moments when I'm listening to music and lifting weights or driving somewhere alone. I seem to relive everything I've done in great detail.

I feel like I've had a full life and done a lot of amazing things, but there was a time that I still felt like I was missing something. I have climbed mountains and spent a night huddled in a snow cave during a blizzard above the tree line. I trekked across a glacier while roped up with my two climbing buddies as it groaned and cracked under our feet. I've explored ghost towns and abandoned mines, including rappelling down into vertical shafts. I've jumped out of a plane at 13,000 feet. I've crossed the North Atlantic twice on a ship during storms raging so bad we had to clip a safety line to the rail while standing watch. I've hiked in the Scottish Highlands and dived in the coral beds off the coast of Cuba. I've passed through the Panama Canal twice.

I've been aboard the USS *Nautilus*, the first nuclear submarine, just before it was decommissioned. I've worked on nuclear submarines and climbed into a 3,000-gallon stainless steel shipboard tank that had previously held radioactive water while wearing an air-fed suit to do a radioactive contamination survey. I've gone solo skiing and backpacking all over the United States. I've been a tank commander and gone barreling across the Mojave Desert at full speed in a tank. I've eaten rattlesnakes cooked over an open fire and flown over the Afghan Hindu Kush in a small plane in the dead of winter.

I'm not trying to brag ... well, maybe a little bit. That's a lot of cool stuff, but I know people who have done even more amazing things. But at least my life was never sheltered. I always looked for the next adventure. But despite everything I'd done, I felt my life wouldn't be complete until I had matched myself against war. The ultimate challenge of courage and determination. At least that's how I saw it. I'm sure some of the people reading this can understand that.

I spent 12 years in the US military: four years in the Navy, and eight years in the Army. I went from an E-1 to an Armor captain. I did a lot of tough training, including four years as an officer in the Soviet-style opposing forces (OPFOR) at the National Training Center in the Mojave Desert. The OPFOR was patterned after a Cold War-era Soviet Motorized Rifle Regiment to give regular US armored units a live opponent to fight against in training. We used some actual Soviet equipment along with visually modified American equipment, and spent well over two hundred days a year in the field in summer heat and winter rain and cold, so the deep desert was nothing new to me.

But all that training felt like it had been for nothing since I'd never been in the right unit at the right time to deploy to war. I felt like a trained ER nurse who'd never worked in an ER. So, when the chance to do private security work in Iraq came along, I didn't hesitate.

In the summer of 2004, while finishing up a PhD degree, I tapped into my network of fellow crazy people to look for a contract gig in either Afghanistan or Iraq. The network came through and by August of that year, I was on a plane for Amman, Jordan, the PhD forgotten, and a security contract in hand. That was the beginning of my two and a half years in Iraq, followed by another 14 or so years doing contract security work worldwide. During those 14 years, I worked gigs on the West Bank, Pakistan, and Kenya. I made multiple trips to Afghanistan and was in Cairo for a front-row seat to the 2011 Arab Spring riots that overthrew Hosni Mubarak. I dealt with everything from terrorist bombings to abductions and even oversaw one company's response to the Haiti earthquake of 2010.

But Iraq was always the high point of my career and to be honest, of my life. It was my full immersion into a country at war, not as a soldier insulated from the people by my uniform and military procedures, but as a civilian security contractor who had to spend a lot of time with the people of Iraq as well as other contractors from all over the world. I saw and did things that people only see and do in movies and video games. Some of those things were gruesome and, in the moment, terrifying. Others were funny, or just left me shaking my head in disbelief. But they were all infinitely worth it and I would do it over again in a heartbeat.

We never considered ourselves mercenaries, although some people called us that, as well as gunslingers, and sometimes worse. It was difficult and dangerous work, and occasionally boring. We lived rough in camps and slept in tents and our vehicles. I was shot at with small arms and rocket-propelled grenades (RPGs), took cover from mortars, and had my vehicle targeted by IEDs (improvised explosive devices) more than once. I was in a high-speed traffic accident and suffered food poisoning … twice. I had teammates, and in some cases people I was responsible for, killed and wounded. I saw other people I knew screwed over by employers who skipped the country in the middle of the night and left them stranded and unpaid like something out of a movie. The money was good, but it was more than the money. I was proud that I was there, and serving my country by protecting innocent American lives in the only role open to me after leaving the military.

Most of the time we barely knew each other's names, so we just called each other by call signs like Nasty, Speedbump, and Casper, and only occasionally by first names. It was simpler that way. Over the years, I've lost track of most of the people I knew while I was there. Some of them may still be working in hot spots around the world. I know many of the South Africans I worked with are. Others have returned home to live a normal, if less interesting life. I will not use anyone's real name as I tell this story to protect everyone's privacy, and because I can't find most of them to get their permission. Call it professional courtesy. I will use real call signs when I can remember them because those can't cause anyone any problems.

Full disclosure: I personally experienced or witnessed the vast majority of the events described in this book. Those few that I was not present for are so noted and were related to me by multiple people I knew and worked with daily. I trust their account of the events to the extent they recall them accurately, although it is always possible that different people saw and experienced the same things in different ways. Of the events I experienced, I will relate them to the best of my recollection. Keeping in mind that most of these events happened some 20 years ago, there is a chance that I might misremember a place name or a small detail. My apologies if that occurs, rest assured it is not intentional.

So, this is my story. If you were there too, some of it may seem familiar to you. If not, then I hope it gives you at least some idea of what it was like to be a private security contractor in Iraq during a long and very dirty insurgent war.

CHAPTER I

Arriving in Iraq

It was a typical mid-August day in the desert back in 2004 as we arrived at Trebil, the border post between Jordan and Iraq. We'd just made the 200-mile drive from Amman, Jordan and the weather was hot and the desert dusty. We'd spent the previous night in a hotel in Amman, eating Arabic food and drinking in the atmosphere. I had sat on a terrace listening to evening prayers being called from a mosque and thinking to myself that this was actually going to happen. I was going to Iraq.

We were originally supposed to fly into Baghdad on a Royal Jordanian flight, the only airline providing regular service into Iraq. However, insurgents were shooting at planes trying to land at Baghdad International Airport (BIAP), and flights were suspended, so we were driving. Our first ride took us as far as the border, where a team from our employer was supposed to meet us. Naturally, they weren't there when we arrived.

The border crossing was crowded with locals trying to go in one direction or the other. It was a genuine mob scene, and my first real exposure to just how chaotic travel in the Middle East is. We didn't have any visible weapons or equipment so we could have been mistaken for tourists, assuming any tourists would be going to Iraq. We didn't see any other Westerners at the crossing, and we had no idea where we were supposed to meet our ride. Eventually, some American troops posted at the border told us we were at the civilian gate and needed to move a few hundred meters to what passed for a military gate. We dragged our gear across the sand to where we settled into a deserted Iraqi border police building and waited. The troops thoughtfully gave us some water and MREs.

After a couple of hours, the team sent by our employer arrived to pick us up. They gave us a quick security briefing and handed out AKs and body armor. Then the seven of us loaded up into soft-skinned Suburbans for the drive to Baghdad.

We made the roughly 300-mile "desert dash" in around six hours. The trip was uneventful, except for stopping once on an overpass where we had a clear field of view to piss by the roadside. We arrived at our "camp" in the early evening. It was some houses on the Radwaniyah side of BIAP. Supposedly, they'd been holiday residences for Saddam's Ba'ath Party cronies. It was a pretty, almost idyllic area with canals and little vacation houses. The canals were all dry now, but there were still a lot of trees and greenery and some wildlife. I found a hedgehog trundling along under a bush. The area was abandoned, so the company had just moved into a few houses. They set up a generator so there would be electricity, but relied on the local plumbing for water, which worked most of the time although the drains backed up a lot. Nobody drank the water; we just used it for everything else. Everyone racked out on army cots. The company had a villa in Baghdad too, but I only spent a few nights there, including one night when what became an internationally known incident occurred just a few doors down the street. I'll get to that later.

So ended my first day as a private security contractor in Iraq. The next two and a half years would be more eventful, but it was a start. It was the last time I entered Iraq by vehicle. After that first trip, I flew into BIAP, and once to Nasiriyah. Most often, I came in on Royal Jordanian Airlines from Amman, but once I came in on a small charter flight from Beirut, Lebanon. You could always tell you were arriving in a war zone because the plane would do a spiral to lose altitude before landing rather than a long gentle glide into the runway patterns. They did the same taking off, spiraling up to rapidly gain altitude. The spiral made it more difficult for insurgents to target the plane with small arms or surface-to-air missiles. It worked most of the time, although a DHL cargo plane was hit by a missile on take-off a few months later.

There were no operational covered concourses at BIAP, so you deplaned by walking down a set of portable stairs pushed up against the plane and onto the tarmac. The first whiff of Iraqi air always smelled like burning rubber and raw sewage. There were usually Nepali Gurkha security guards standing around with AKs. Everything was covered with a layer of dust and there were still bullet holes in the airport terminal windows. It was like walking into another world, and it wasn't a place everybody felt comfortable. One day three new guys flew in for security contracts. They got off the plane, took one look around, and said it wasn't what they were expecting. They took the same plane back to Jordan when it left an hour later. I'm not sure what they were expecting; it was a war zone after all.

Except for a few weeks out of the country between contracts or on R&R, I was in Iraq almost continually from August 2004 to April 2007. During that time, I worked on various contacts as a PSD (personal security detail) team member, doing convoy escort, as the security manager of a remote reconstruction project on the Euphrates River, and as the in-country senior security manager for a large Department of Defense (DoD) reconstruction contractor with projects all over the country.

I enjoyed all my gigs in Iraq. All were different, and they all had their ups and downs. Each of them had moments that were deadly boredom, and moments that were just deadly. I was amazed at how much time I spent sitting. Sitting in camp, sitting in vehicles, and just sitting around waiting. You had to work to find a way to get some exercise, finding a gym on a base, or doing calisthenics in your room. There was no place to go for runs or even walks, although the retired South African sergeant major of our static guard force and I used to kit up and walk around the 400-acre construction site every day when I was in Nasiriyah, just to keep an eye on things. I was probably in better shape the first day I arrived in Iraq than I was the day I left. But I never once regretted being there, no matter what was or was not happening. It was a time that fundamentally changed me.

What is a Private Security Contractor?

"In a good mercenary outfit, they're all there because they want to be. All right, the motive is probably the high money they earn, but they all want to do it. They're all volunteers."

COL. "MAD" MIKE HOARE

I suppose that in any book about, or even any discussion of private security contractors, it is beneficial to clarify just who we are and what it is we do. As I have said elsewhere in this book, we are not mercenaries, although we were often called that. Mercenaries provide a private army. They work for the highest bidder to conduct military operations that include both offensive and defensive missions.

Private security contractors provide protection. They protect organizations, facilities, materials, pipelines, ships, and especially, people. They sometimes work as individuals who contract directly with the client, but more often they work as part of a team the client contracts for from a company that provides security services. I have worked both as an individual and as part of a contracted team. In Iraq, I generally worked with a team.

Make no mistake, international private security work pays well. I'm not talking about security guard work. Most security guards are not well trained, and the work doesn't pay very well. I'm talking about people, mostly with prior military experience, who have skills that enable them to function effectively in a high-risk environment. Professionals who can protect other people and critical sites from organized terrorists, cartels, and even paramilitary groups at high risk to themselves. It is important to understand that the private security contractors did not just go to Iraq and try to drum up business. They were there because it was a formal policy of the U.S. Department of Defense to tell reconstruction contractors that the Army could not and would not protect them. If they wanted to work on reconstruction projects in Iraq, they had to provide their own security, and the only way to do that was to hire private security contractors to protect their people and projects. It wasn't a job for the average mall cop. It was a hostile environment in an active conflict zone and hard professionals were needed.

In my time in Iraq, I worked with people who were former US Army soldiers, Rangers, Green Berets, and former Marines. I worked with guys who were veterans of the British Army and Royal Marines, Army of South Africa, Rhodesian Army, Angolan Army, Nepali Army, Iraqi Army, Lebanese Christian Militia, and Kurdish Peshmerga among others. I even knew one German guy who was a former member of the French Foreign Legion. A great many of them were combat veterans. They were all tough, dependable people who I trusted with my life. If they were good enough to get a private security contract with the teams I worked on, they were good. One thing we all had in common was that we were exactly where we wanted to be. We came to Iraq by choice, and even though we knew we could get on the next plane home if we decided to leave, we stayed there. The people in the military had volunteered to join, but they had been ordered to Iraq and couldn't leave until they received orders telling them to. We were there because it was where we wanted to be. Although we were called mercenaries and gunslingers by both the military and other civilian contractors, that's not how we saw ourselves.

While in Iraq, I worked on PSD (private security detail) teams, did convoy security for shipments of weapons from the United States military to the Iraqi security forces, security management for multiple sites, and finally worked as a site security manager for a remote project in southern Iraq. They were all different, but they all had some aspects that were the same and required the same skills.

CHAPTER 2

Private Security Details

As the name implies, a private security detail (PSD) team provides security for people. Where close protection teams primarily focus on dismounted security, a PSD team specializes in mobile security. In other words, security while the principal or clients are moving from one place to another, although they also provide security for the clients while they are on-site. PSD teams usually work in high-risk regions like Latin America, the Middle East, and Africa, and almost all the team members have a military background.

All the PSD teams I worked on consisted of nine guys and three vehicles, two up-armored Suburbans, and a B6-rated armored SUV for the clients. If you needed more room for clients, you added another whole team, not just another vehicle. An up-armored SUV has armor plates installed in the doors and body panels, an armored tub built into the rear cargo space, and armored shutters over the side windows. The roof is unarmored, and the window glass is just regular glass, so the level of protection is limited.

The B6 client vehicle has been armored at a special factory. B6 is a rating designated by the US National Institute of Justice that tells you at a glance how heavily the vehicle is armored. A B6 vehicle has armored plate installed to shield the entire passenger compartment, including the roof and floor. It also has bulletproof windows, and sometimes even run-flat tires that can go for miles after being shot out. The armor will stop a bullet from a .30 caliber sniper rifle and mitigate the effects of an IED blast to an extent. The windows do not open, so riding in one is like being inside a steel box. They are very heavy, around 10,000 pounds, so driving one is different from driving the family SUV. They handle differently and they are much easier to roll over.

The team usually consists of nine people. The lead vehicle is up-armored and has three guys in it: the driver, a man in the front passenger seat, and a shooter in the back seat behind the driver. The client vehicle has the principals and two PSD team members: the driver and the team leader. The last vehicle is the other up-armored SUV. It has four people in it: the driver, a man in the front passenger seat, a shooter in the back seat behind the driver, and a machine gunner facing out the back. The guy in the back is usually referred to as the "trunk monkey." Movements are limited to no more than three clients to one team. That's because if the client's vehicle is disabled, three clients plus the two team members who were in the client vehicle are all that can be transferred to the other team vehicles. There isn't room for any more people and you can't leave anyone behind on the road when you move on to get the clients to safety.

At least that was the ideal. As I will explain in a subsequent chapter, my first contract was with a company that hadn't invested the money to provide us with up-armored SUVs. Instead, we drove around Iraq in standard soft-skinned Suburbans, although the clients were in B6 vehicles. Fortunately, I was in up-armored vehicles on my subsequent contracts, but in those early days of the occupation of Iraq, things were a little less structured.

Since SUVs aren't as common in Iraq as they are in the United States, PSD teams tended to stand out, making them easier to target. For this reason, some companies chose to run in armored sedans instead of SUVs. As sedans are much easier to immobilize than an SUV, they relied on keeping a low profile and not being identified as a PSD team. I never liked the idea of using armored sedans. A vehicle parked to block the road, a few chunks of broken concrete, or even a hole in the road can immobilize a sedan. Plus, an SUV can easily go over a curb or off the side of the road to avoid a problem, but a sedan is stuck, which is not a good situation if you are being shot at or people are trying to get at your clients.

PSD teams rely on movement, usually fast movement, to avoid and escape threats like ambushes and abductions. We'll fight if there is no other choice, but the main goal is to get the clients out of the danger zone. Everything was seen as a threat. If a car pulled out in front of you, it might be an attempt to slow or stop the team. If a pedestrian walked out in front of you, it might be an attempt to slow or stop the team. That may seem radical, but given the propensity for Islamic extremists to embrace martyrdom, anything was possible. We used whatever tactics and standard procedures we could to keep moving. If your vehicle was disabled, you put it in neutral so the vehicle behind you could push you out of the kill zone. You always carried a tow strap hooked up to the rear of your vehicle so that if you had to tow another vehicle, all you had to do was get in front of it and hook it up. You could be gone in under a minute.

In my time on the PSD contracts, our teams were attacked with small arms fire, IEDs, and other vehicles trying to run them off the road. Another big risk was traffic accidents. PSD teams move fast to make it more difficult for the bad guys to catch them in an ambush or trigger an IED at the moment they are passing it, so high-speed accidents were a genuine risk. We had several PSD team members wounded but we never had a client seriously injured. We got the job done.

CHAPTER 3

Convoy Security

Escorting convoys is very different from PSD work. The ones we escorted were not the usual run-of-the-mill convoys carrying food or kitchen equipment; there were all sorts on the roads of Iraq during the war and occupation. Everything traveled by convoys, from food for the dining facilities (DFACS) to goods for the American PXs. The convoys we escorted all originated out of the warehouse complex at Abu Ghraib and transported highly sensitive equipment that was being provided from the United States to the Iraqi security forces. We escorted trucks loaded with weapons, ammunition, military equipment, police equipment, and medical supplies. We even escorted trucks loaded with police cars and armored vehicles. All things the insurgents would have loved to get their hands on, or barring that, destroy.

Convoy security is a lower-prestige job than PSD work. It's also a much higher-risk job. Where PSD teams can easily choose and vary routes as the situation dictates, that's not something you can do with a convoy of 10 semi-trucks driven by poorly skilled Iraqis. You must use routes that the trucks can negotiate quickly and without a lot of stops, usually between Abu Ghraib and whatever Iraqi base or supply hub you were going to. All places that were easy to watch. We were certain that every insurgent within 100 miles knew exactly when a convoy of guns and ammo left Abu Ghraib.

Another factor is speed, or the lack of it. PSD teams tend to go fast to make triggering an ambush more difficult for the bad guys. You can't do that with a convoy of trucks. You are limited to the speed of the slowest truck to keep the convoy together. That makes it an easy target.

All the insurgents need to do to interdict a convoy is disable one truck to stop the whole thing. A PSD team can abandon a disabled vehicle and get the client out of the kill zone, even if they have to transfer vehicles. We couldn't abandon a disabled truck, we had to defend it. You don't leave a truck loaded with hundreds of AKs and thousands of rounds of ammunition for the bad guys to collect.

The truck drivers were largely Iraqis, although there were a few from Bangladesh. How they ended up driving their own truck in Iraq is anybody's guess. The US said it was trying to support independent Iraqi truckers by giving them contracts to haul the sensitive cargo carried by the convoys we escorted. The running joke among us was that the Iraqis became independent truckers by stealing the trucks that were abandoned during the invasion the year before. Many of the trucks were still painted in the official colors of the Iraqi government transportation ministry.

Suffice it to say that these guys weren't the kind of professional truckers we think of in the United States. Like everything else in Iraq, they were mostly self-taught and felt successful if they could get the truck moving and actually arrive at their destination.

The logistics of trying to move anywhere from four to 16 tractor-trailer trucks on the congested city highways and remote desert roads of Iraq was fraught with difficulties and gave the insurgents plenty of opportunities to ambush us. The trucks were often slow, and the rest of the convoy was only as fast as the slowest truck. Breakdowns were common since the Iraqis were responsible for maintaining their trucks. We even had one spontaneously catch on fire one day. The drivers weren't very good at securing their loads, resulting in items falling off the flatbed trucks. We had to stop one time because a dozen cases of AK rifles fell off and burst open on the road. We spent the next 30 minutes scrambling around picking them up and trying to get the wooden cases put back together enough to secure them back on the trailer.

All this made escorting convoys difficult and dangerous. We had to ride herd on the convoy trucks, as well as keep the other traffic away from them, often by interposing our trucks between the semis and whatever was approaching them. To do this we had up-armored Ford F350 Crew Cab trucks. They had armor in the doors with armored shutters over the windows, and an armored tub in the bed. The roofs and windshields were unarmored.

Each truck had a crew of four to five men. There was one American who was the vehicle commander and drove the truck since we didn't trust our Kurds to do that. There were also three to four Kurdish Peshmerga shooters; one in the front passenger seat covering the right side, one in the back seat behind the driver covering the left side, and one in the bed unless the truck also had a machine gun, in which case there were two. Since my truck usually had Casper, our former Lebanese Christian Militia interpreter on board, he took the place of the Kurd who would normally ride shotgun. More about Casper later.

It was dangerous work, and we had several fatalities on the teams. Everyone lived two to a room in the camp prefabs, so each room had two name plaques on the door with the occupants' names on them. When someone was killed in action, their name plaque would be removed from their door and mounted over the door leading from the operations center to the outside assembly area. There were six plaques with expats' names on them and several more with the names of Kurdish team members over that door. People were killed and injured by small arms, IEDs, and traffic accidents. On the upside, the trucks were all brand new, and we were issued excellent weapons, equipment, and even uniforms by the company. Everything was first class, and the pay was good.

CHAPTER 4

Security Management and Site Security

Security management and site security are by far the least exciting of all the tasks private security contractors take on. That's not to say they don't have interesting and sometimes dangerous aspects, just that overall, they are calmer than being out on the road. I will relate some of the specific experiences and problems that I experienced in other chapters, but for now, I'll just give a quick overview of what these tasks involve.

Security management in a high-risk overseas environment consists of creating the tactics, techniques, and procedures (TTP) your security teams will use to get the job done, both for the camps and job sites, and when your people go outside the wire. It also involves reviewing all the tasks your clients must perform in their contracts and deciding when and how to get them there and back safely. There are also investigations and after-action reviews of incidents to determine how they occurred and how to prevent them from occurring in the future, or at least reduce the impact since some things are beyond your control. There's more, but that's the gist of it. In short, you are responsible for everything that happens.

Site security is specific to a particular site. In my case, it was a very large construction project in southern Iraq. The site covered 400 acres and employed around 400 local construction workers, plus another 30 or so expat engineers and construction managers. I had two South African PSD teams on-site and around 20 Nepalese static guards. We were isolated and there was no way any help was going to reach us in an emergency in under two hours. The camp was fortified with HESCO barriers, sandbags, bunkers, and guard towers, most of which I laid out. We had a couple of incidents of being shot at with RPGs and small arms, and there were myriad security problems daily. Everything from the locals threatening to kill us all because we'd blocked off a trail cutting through the site that had been in use for God knows how long, to local criminals trying to shake down the employees on-site, to the Mahdi militia threatening to overrun us. There were also all sorts of political issues where we had to make nice with everyone, from the local Iraqi security forces to the tribal sheiks from the surrounding villages. It's a 24-hour job with no downtime.

All told, high-risk security contracting has a lot of facets, all of which benefit from military experience. Leadership, organization, logistics, and tactics all come into play. Some positions are more dangerous than others, and some pay more. No matter which one you are doing, it is a lot more interesting than any other civilian job I ever had.

We're Not in Kansas Anymore

I'd lived in seven states and traveled around quite a bit before going to Iraq; mostly in the military to Central America and Scotland, plus a few trips to Canada, which was about the same as being in the US. Overall, I'd traveled enough to know things were going to be different in the Middle East than they were anyplace else. The fact that I was going to even a low-intensity war zone added some spice to the mix.

But there were a few milestones that told me things were going to be more different in Iraq than I realized. It was more than just the people and the scenery looking different from what I was used to, it was the entire personality of both the country and its people. No matter what the specifics were, as a whole, the differences were almost surreal at times.

CHAPTER 5

The Souk

It was August and hot, so the company gave us some time to acclimate for the first few days after I and the cluster of new guys who came in with me arrived in Iraq. I'd spent over three years at the National Training Center at Fort Irwin in the Mojave Desert, so I was used to heat, but it was still pretty hot. A couple of the guys who had been there a while took us around to the base PX and then into the Green Zone to do some sightseeing.

One of the places we explored was a souk in the Green Zone. Souk is the Arabic word for an open market or bazaar. There were lots of tents with locals selling everything from food to tourist junk like local clothes and brass bowls. I bought a crappy knife and a couple of keffiyehs, the headscarf Arab men wear that engendered the negative sobriquet "rag heads." To be honest, anyone who has ever spent much time under the hot Middle Eastern sun understands exactly why a keffiyeh is beneficial, and it was funny seeing guys who called the locals rag heads putting bandanas and keffiyehs over their heads to keep their necks from getting sunburned. Mostly I just wandered around looking at all the strange stuff and interesting people.

The locals were super friendly, probably mainly because they wanted us to spend money, which we did. I didn't realize it at the time, but I was lucky to get to go there when I did. Three days later, the place was bombed. Insurgents planted a bomb under one of the booths. It went off when the place was full of people, both foreign and local. It killed a Fijian contractor and a couple of locals and wounded quite a few more people. The Coalition military shut down the souk and it never reopened since it was decided that it was too juicy of a target for bombings. People thought the Green Zone was safe, but it really wasn't. There were multiple incidents there, including American military members being shot on the street.

It made me sad to think of all the smiling people I'd seen at the souk, buying and selling and just enjoying the day. The vendors were happy to have some customers, especially customers like Americans, who had plenty of money to spend and didn't hesitate to do so. The contractors were just enjoying the sights and experience of something they were unlikely to see in America. And it was all ended by a bomb motivated by hate and designed to hurt and maim people who never intended the bomber any harm at all. But that was typical of the war in Iraq where indiscriminate bombings were common, and I would get used to it. After a while, you just got numb to seeing the bits and pieces of automobiles that had been car bombs at the checkpoints and intersections. Especially when you understood and accepted that, but for a matter of timing, the explosion might have occurred when you were there.

CHAPTER 6

Baghdad's Best Filipino-Run Chinese Restaurant

Around the same week as the trip to the souk, some of the guys said there was a Chinese restaurant run by some Filipinos in the Green Zone that was pretty good. Americans like to go out to eat, but in Iraq, contractors either ate at the DFAC or they ate MREs (meals ready to eat), so having someplace to go out to eat was a welcome luxury. A Chinese restaurant sounded good, so around 10 of us loaded up and went looking for it.

There was no sign announcing its location, but fortunately, one of the guys who'd been there before knew how to find it. He led us down a trash- and rubble-choked alley between the original Iraqi-built walls around the houses and the concrete T-walls installed by the military. Eventually, we reached a single Chinese paper lantern hung from a pole. The place looked like a hole in the wall from the outside. There was trash and debris from the battles a few months earlier still scattered around, and the ever-present Iraqi dust made a thick coating on everything.

It was in a residential home that had been cleared out and converted into a restaurant. I was still getting used to how spartan the insides of Iraqi buildings were. The floors are all some kind of tiles and the walls are stark white. There are rarely any pictures on the walls, and they don't have carpets on the floors, probably because they would be too hard to keep clean with all the dirt and dust in the air. It felt like we were sitting down inside an abandoned building.

We all got cans of Coke and little one-page paper menus. I don't remember what I ordered but it wasn't bad. As I looked around, the incongruity of the situation struck me. Here was a bunch of Americans in Baghdad, Iraq sitting in a Chinese restaurant run by Filipinos while outside there were still piles of rubble and bombed-out buildings. Not quite an "Alice down the rabbit hole" moment, but things would only get stranger.

CHAPTER 7

Welcome to Iraq!

My first PSD mission came a few days later. We were tasked with taking three of our clients to a meeting at the Iraqi Ministry of Water (MOW) out in the city. My team leader, I'll call him Javier, was a former Green Beret originally born in Panama. We went from our camp outside of Radwaniyah into the Green Zone to pick up the clients, then out one of the many gates and into the city. It was a trip the team had made multiple times.

I had arrived in Iraq by driving across the desert from Amman, Jordan, so by then, I was used to the chaos of traffic in the Middle East. But it was different when I knew that we might be attacked because some locals wanted to kill our clients. The city was incredibly congested. There were people and scooters going every which way and the traffic was going in every direction. The streets were lined with shops and businesses, and the areas in front of the stores were stacked with goods for sale like outdoor markets. There were no sidewalks on most of the streets, and the atmosphere was chaotic. As I sat there in the back seat of the Suburban, facing sideways out the open window with my AK across my lap so it wouldn't be visible, it's no exaggeration to say I was hypervigilant.

We arrived after around 30 minutes of slow progress through the city. The MOW was in a walled compound with machine-gun towers on the corners. The guards waved us through, and we pulled into the circular drive by the entrance. The lead vehicle pulled diagonally across the driveway to block anyone from coming in that way, and then the client B6 vehicle stopped behind it. The clients would stay in the vehicle until one of us got them out. We were the trail vehicle, and we pulled in at an angle behind the B6 to block the drive from behind and provide cover for the clients. The team leader got them out and we formed a diamond formation to escort them to the entrance. The local guards didn't want all of us to go in, so the team leader assigned someone to go in with them to keep us in the loop, and the rest of us found places to stand or sit and wait.

About 20 minutes after we arrived, there was a commotion out on the street, but the sliding steel gate was closed, so we couldn't see what was going on. There were several muffled explosions and the ground shook, then one of the towers ripped off a burst from its Russian 12.7 machine gun. We took cover with half of us watching the gate and the rest watching the guys in the tower since we really didn't trust them. Other than some smoke and dust filtering over the wall, things settled down after a few minutes. Javier grinned, clapped me on the shoulder, and said, "Welcome to Iraq!" I grinned and told him I was happy to be there.

We never did find out what was going on, but it didn't really matter anyway since it was all over by the time the meeting finished and we headed back to the Green Zone. There was some debris on the street and a couple of craters in the wall where whatever blew up had hit them. It was probably a couple of RPGs, but they didn't penetrate the stone and brick. People watch movies and think RPGs set off these huge explosions, but that's not how they work. They're designed to penetrate the metal armor on tanks and infantry fighting vehicles. When the rocket grenade detonates, it creates a small cone of metal that burns through the armor. They do explode, but they usually don't blow down entire walls. The trip back was more of the same as the trip there, chaotic but uneventful. We dropped the clients off at their camp then went back to our camp and then to chow. A little excitement, but nothing unusual to the guys who had been there a while. Still, it was interesting, and I enjoyed it. So ended my first working day in Iraq.

CHAPTER 8

Recon by Goat Truck

Guerrilla wars are different from the depictions of war you see in movies where there is a discernable front line and areas behind the lines are relatively safe. Iraq was an insurgency, a guerrilla war where the "enemy" was all around you and there was no way to tell them from the innocent civilians. Trust was in short supply. By then, there had been too many bombings, abductions, and ambushes.

A couple of weeks after the MOW mission, a couple of the guys were assigned to do a recce to check out the routes in a new AO (area of operations). We weren't the Army, so we didn't have armored vehicles and large formations of heavily armed men and women to run patrols in unfamiliar areas to get the lay of the land. So, we had to be more creative. I was still relatively new, and it only called for two guys, so I didn't get to go on the actual mission, but it brought home just how strange the situation was and the need for a paradigm shift in my outlook on the world I had willingly put myself into.

A couple of the senior guys with beards dressed in local clothes, then scrounged up one of those beat-up white Toyota Hilux trucks that were everywhere in Iraq and went low profile. No ball caps or sunglasses. To add to the illusion, they bought a goat and tied it to a ring in the bed of the truck so it could stand there and look authentic.

Their disguises probably wouldn't have stood up to close scrutiny, but they were fine for the quick glances they would receive as they drove past the locals. Just a couple of farmers taking a goat somewhere. I thought it was a good plan and it went off just fine. They drove the routes the PSD teams would be traveling in the coming weeks, making note of the quickest routes and danger spots like choke points. They left in the morning and were back by midafternoon. The goat was barbecued the next day.

Overall, my first couple of weeks in-country lived up to what I was hoping to experience in Iraq. It was fulfilling to finally use my skills for real, and even better than that, I was having fun. The next couple of years would bring more experiences, both good and bad, but it was a good start.

Colorful Characters

One of the most interesting and entertaining aspects of international private security contracting is the people you meet along the way. Most of the guys you work around are hard-charging alpha males, or else they wouldn't be risking their lives when they didn't have to. But some truly colorful characters stood out during my time in Iraq, even in a crowd of people who stood out. These are the kind of guys who would have signed on with Colonel "Mad" Mike Hoare 20 or 30 years ago—the kind of guys who went off to join the Foreign Legion. The kind of guys who signed contracts that put them in the middle of a very dirty guerrilla war.

Most of the Americans were younger guys, maybe in their late 20s and early 30s, although there were some older guys like me, too. Many of them were coming off active duty in the US military. Everything from Marine snipers to Army Rangers, along with a lot of guys who were just good honest grunts. But many of the guys from outside the US were older and had background stories right out of an adventure novel. Some were there for the money. Others were adrenalin junkies. A few were there because they didn't fit in anywhere else. Many were there because they were bored and wanted adventure. I fit into that category. And really, to many of us, adventure was what it was all about.

CHAPTER 9

An Irishman in Baghdad

Getting a flight out of Baghdad International Airport (BIAP) was an exercise in both determination and patience. The only airline providing service was Royal Jordanian. I got an Iraqi Air flight out once, but Iraqi Air didn't fly very often so Royal Jordanian was pretty much it. Besides, none of us really trusted the airworthiness of the old Iraqi Air planes. Because of all the risks, and the fact that Baghdad airport didn't operate after sundown, Royal Jordanian had strict rules for scheduling flights. All the flights took place in daylight and planes never stayed in Baghdad overnight. The flights from Amman usually arrived anytime between 10:00 am and 1:00 pm, and always left again by 3:00 pm. If there was any kind of a delay affecting a flight into Iraq that might result in a plane being at BIAP after dark, the flight was simply canceled with no advance notice and the plane never left Jordan. When that happened, you were left sitting around at the airport with no idea what was going on.

And there were plenty of delays. Everything from sand and dust storms to people shooting at the planes. We were able to get tickets in advance through our admin people, but there was no way of knowing the status of the flight, so you just showed up at the airport and hoped for the best. There were no announcements or status boards, or any other way of checking on flights, so you just sat around waiting.

Most of the time you just hung around in the unsecured portion of the terminal, although there was a lounge once you got through the first set of turnstiles. Once I sat in the lounge waiting for a flight that was supposed to take off at 1:00 pm. The plane never showed up and no one ever told us what was going on. Finally, around 5:00 pm, we ventured out into the main airport area to see what was up, only to find that all the airport workers had gone home leaving us sitting there. At times there would be hundreds of people crowded around the entry turnstiles, some standing, most sitting on the floor.

It was during one of these long waits of several hours that I met an Irish guy who was also a security contractor, I'll call him Conor. He had a great Irish accent and was very talkative, so talking with him was a good way to pass the time. Conor had a scar across his throat. Not a little scar, but a long one that went from below his right ear to below his left ear. Exactly the kind of scar a person would have if someone had tried to cut his throat. I didn't ask him about it during the few hours that we sat around eating junk food and talking; it's not the sort of thing you ask someone you barely know about.

He was a funny guy and made a lot of self-disparaging jokes about Irishmen. A young American woman was waiting in the crowd near us. She was a journalism student who was there on some kind of apprenticeship. During the conversation, she commented that one of her professors at her university back home was Irish. The Irishman burst out laughing and said she must not have gone to a very good university if they allowed an Irishman to teach there. We all laughed, but she clearly didn't know how to react to him.

We talked about the British military, and it became evident that the guy was a former member of the SAS, the British special operations unit officially called the Special Air Service. They are some of the toughest operators in the world, and the SAS was the inspiration for America's Operational Detachment Delta. He didn't go into any details about previous missions he had been on. Guys that are the real deal rarely do. They don't have to because they have nothing to prove to anybody, especially themselves. Conor talked about the SAS and its history, including a guy named Paddy Mayne. Paddy Mayne was an Irish member of the British Royal Army who served under the famous Captain David Stirling in the SAS during World War II. In fact, he was one of the founding members of the 1st SAS Regiment and fought the Germans and Italians in the desert during the North African campaign. He was known as a hard-fighting and hard-drinking man and was one of the British Army's most highly-decorated soldiers. Mayne was recruited into the SAS while sitting in a jail cell for striking a superior officer, served heroically during the war as a special operator, and died after the war in a drunk driving accident. Just the kind of person you would expect an Irish mercenary fighting in a war in the desert to admire, and Conor was quite passionate about Paddy Mayne and the history of the SAS. I guess we got along pretty well, because he suddenly dug into his carry-on bag and pulled out a book about Paddy Mayne. He handed it to me and told me to keep it and read it. I did and I still have it sitting on my bookshelf. It is a very good book.

CHAPTER 10

Dandre and the Terrorists

Practically all of the South Africans working in Iraq were white and spoke Afrikaans, that cool-sounding Dutch derivative language they speak in South Africa. They had all served in the South African Army or police commando units during previous decades, and many were veterans of the war with Angola and the terrorism that was raging before apartheid ended. I am not making any kind of statement or judgment in telling you that, just letting you know their experience and backgrounds.

One of the South Africans I worked with was an older guy whom I will call Dandre. Dandre was at least in his 50s but he was slender and fit. His hair and well-groomed beard were grey. He was pleasant and soft-spoken, but something about him said that he was not someone to be taken lightly. He didn't talk much about his past, many of the South Africans didn't, although a few were pretty open about it. The South African military was small, and they all knew each other from long before they came to Iraq. One of the other South Africans, that I was pretty good friends with, told a couple of us about Dandre's past.

He had been a senior officer in a South African special forces commando unit. His orders were to track down and apprehend terrorists under the 1967 Terrorism Act passed by the apartheid government. South Africa was a very violent place in the 1970s and 1980s. Organizations like the Umkhonto we Sizwe carried out bombings, guerrilla warfare, and other terrorist acts against the government and the death and damage toll was high. Atrocities were committed by both sides during that violent period in South Africa. Again, I'm not passing judgment on either side, just setting up the environment Dandre worked in.

The special forces commando unit Dandre commanded had been tasked with capturing three men who were suspected of numerous bombings, abductions, murders, and attacks on police and white South Africans. He knew who they were and had no doubt that they were guilty. But the men were not stupid and were well insulated from the acts through a cell system that protected their identities from any legally admissible evidence of the violence. It was very frustrating for Dandre and his elite team of anti-terrorist commandos. They knew these three men were guilty of ordering and carrying out attacks that had killed people and destroyed property throughout the country, but they could not get enough evidence to arrest them and have them convicted. Unless they could catch them in the act, they couldn't arrest them, and they weren't likely to catch them in the act.

Dandre and his men knew this violence was ongoing and that the longer the men were free the more trouble they would cause. They were desperate to stop the carnage, and that desperation pushed them over the line. They decided to act on their own. Dandre's unit was highly competent and capturing the three men was an easy matter. But, once Dandre's unit had them, they knew they had to neutralize them in a way that couldn't be traced back to them. They wouldn't be taking them to prison or turning them over to the courts. So, they conceived a plan to get rid of them permanently. They drugged the three men and put them into a car. Then they set the car on fire and rolled it off a cliff so it would look like an accident.

This isn't the kind of story you take at face value, so we decided to do a little digging. Since we had been told about it, that meant the story wasn't a secret anymore. We knew that South Africa had set up the Truth and Reconciliation Commission in 1996 to bring past crimes against human rights into the light and, in some cases, grant amnesty to the perpetrators and offer reparation and rehabilitation to the victims. It was established by none other than Nelson Mandela and overseen by Archbishop Desmond Tutu. The transcripts of the Truth and Reconciliation Commission hearings are available online. Since we had Dandre's full name and the basic facts of the story, we were able to find the actual transcript of the testimonies given in the hearings, and we verified that it was indeed a true story. We never looked at Dandre quite the same way after that.

That was a horrific period in South Africa's history and something most Americans can't begin to understand. People on both sides of the conflict felt justified in their actions and it had the potential to create a rift in South African society that could have torn the country apart. I give the government a lot of credit for setting up the reconciliation process and hopefully bringing some closure to the situation. But it left a lot of people in a position where, although they had expressed remorse for their actions and been granted amnesty, they were still known to have committed them, making them potential pariahs in their own country. Iraq was a good place to leave that behind.

CHAPTER 11

The Legionnaire

I've honestly lost track of how many times I've been to Amman, Jordan. It's a nice town and I've run around the city quite a bit. At one point I was even met at the airport by the former commander of King Hussein's personal bodyguard. He was retired by then and he was working as our local contact for a close protection (CP) gig. It was evident he was still known and respected … or feared by the security people. He met me at the gate after my plane landed and walked me right through all the incoming security, and the visa process. Every security person in the airport recognized him and just nodded respectfully when we came through. He even got us all handguns to use while we were doing the CP job, even though we technically weren't authorized to carry them in Jordan.

It was on a different trip through Amman that I met another of the colorful people I encountered on my travels. There were three of us killing time at the airport until our plane would leave the next morning. We had 12 hours to wait and didn't feel like getting a room at a hotel, so we were sitting on the floor in the terminal talking and dozing. I noticed a Westerner walking around, obviously killing time too. He was wearing a sleeveless T-shirt, and I noticed his tattoo. It was a skull with a stylized grenade that is unique among military badges. If that wasn't enough, it had *Légion étrangère* written above and below it. There was only one thing it could be.

I walked over to him and asked if he had served in the Legion. There's only one Legion, and that is the French Foreign Legion, of course. He smiled and said he had, then asked if I had. I told him no, but that I recognized his tattoo, and it was an honor to meet him. Turns out he was a German from Dusseldorf (I'll call him Heinz) who had spent several years in *la Légion étrangère*. These days he was doing contract security work in Iraq, just like the rest of us. I had no doubt he was the real deal. You don't run around with a Legion tattoo unless you earned it, not if you don't want to get stomped into the dirt if you run across a real Legionnaire who figured out you were faking it.

We spent the next 12 hours just hanging out in the airport and talking. At one point he bought us all pizza. His stories were great entertainment to someone like me, someone to whom the French Foreign Legion was almost so cool it had mythical significance. People don't think of France as a militarily active country, and they especially don't realize just how often the Foreign Legion is deployed. Heinz had served in the Gulf War as part of *Opération Daguet* as a member of the 6th Foreign Infantry Regiment (6e REI), making the dash into Iraq at the far-left flank of the entire coalition force to cut off the retreat of Saddam Hussein's forces occupying Kuwait. It was quite a run, and the Legion was in the thick of it. He had also spent time in in Côte d'Ivoire, one of the former French colonial African countries. Like many Europeans, he spoke several languages. In fact, all new Legionnaires are required to learn French.

One of the romanticisms about the Foreign Legion is that they take anyone who can pass the entrance exams. Their website specifically states that "murders, drug trafficking, or other really serious crimes are NOT tolerated," but lesser offenses do not disqualify you. Citizenship, religion, race, social status and pretty much everything else don't matter. Heinz joined because of a bad marriage and boredom, which were the same reasons a lot of the guys I worked with were in Iraq.

We kept in touch for several years after we both left Iraq. He eventually set up a team of guys doing close protection and PSD work, mainly in Eastern Europe. I last heard from him in 2009. His team was providing close protection services to exiled Haitian former President Jean-Bertrand Aristide. He said they were considering coming to the United States and then trying to get him back into Haiti from there. He wanted to know if I could help him obtain rifles and pistols for his team after they entered the United States. I explained that I was working for a U.S. government contractor, and there was no way I could help him with anything like that, even if it was done legally and above board. He said no worries, that they would go through another avenue.

I heard from him a few more times. He had remarried (he was getting a divorce at the time I first met him) and his wife told me he was gone a lot on CP missions to Eastern Europe. I have no idea where he is now, but I hope he's doing well.

CHAPTER 12

The Car Theft Ring

Not everybody I worked with in Iraq had stellar personal values. One such person was a South African I'll call Danie. Danie was a static guard commander. That meant that he oversaw the Angolans who were working as static guards at our client's compound in the Green Zone. He was a bit of a grandstander and he was always looking for ways to look good and get credit for doing a great job, whether he was doing one or not.

At one point, he set his guards to conducting a detailed security sweep of the compound, which included searching under the prefab trailers that served as living quarters for the expat construction engineers living there. An hour into the sweep he came to us with what he called an explosive device he said one of his guys had found. The device consisted of a reasonably small quantity of what looked like propellant for artillery shells tightly wrapped in several layers of heavy paper and cardboard. While the explosive charges from the warheads of artillery rounds make good bombs, the propellant isn't as volatile. It was an odd choice of material for an IED, and wouldn't have had much of an effect even if it had been ignited. There was considerable doubt that it was a legitimate find. In fact, we all quietly believed that Danie had planted it there himself so that his guys could find it and make him look good.

However, shortly after that incident, Danie did actually come to my rescue, so to speak. I had gotten to know a local family who lived near our compound. They were dirt poor and lived in a tiny mud brick house. The father was dead, and the mother and her children lived in poverty. The electricity to their home didn't work, so they had no lights and no refrigerator to store food in the 110-degree heat. I got a hold of some Air Force engineers I knew and got them to come over and repair the power box at their house so they had electricity. It didn't take long for their neighbors to find out they had power and to come over dragging wires they intended to hook up to the box to get juice to their own houses.

I understood that all the other locals needed electricity too, but that would have quickly overwhelmed the box and wiring, and the power would have quit working again. I stopped the other locals from hooking up, which they didn't like at all. Soon, I found myself facing off with a dozen angry Iraqis who were getting loud and making threats. I had a .45 caliber handgun, but it wouldn't have done me much good in that situation. Fortunately, Danie and one of the Angolan guards showed up with their AKs, which immediately got the locals to leave with both me and the little family's power intact. Score one for Danie. But his need to put one over on people finally caught up with him, and the end of his time in Iraq came about a month later.

Expats came and went a lot in Iraq. Contracts ended, people changed jobs, and some people just had enough and went home. That resulted in a lot of vehicles left sitting around. The PX parking lot in the Green Zone was full of dust-covered late-model SUVs and sedans that had been parked and then abandoned when the person who had been driving them left. They all belonged to various government contractors, but it was easy to lose track of them, so it's likely no one even knew where they were. Danie, being the enterprising individual that he was, got the bright idea to develop a partnership with some locals who had legitimate access to the Green Zone for their businesses to make some extra money. The locals would show up with a truck to collect the vehicles Danie would point out to them, and then take them out in the city to sell on the black market. Then they would split the take with Danie.

Normally, nobody paid much attention when an Iraqi truck showed up and winched an abandoned car up onto the bed and took it away. Likewise, no one checked vehicles leaving the secure areas to go out into the city. Danie's scheme worked like a champ ... for a while. But then Army CID caught wind of the same Iraqi truck showing up repeatedly at the PX parking lot, and other locations in the Green Zone, and taking one late-model vehicle after another away for parts unknown. They staked out the lot and confronted the Iraqis when they showed up and started winching a car up onto their truck. Not wanting to get in trouble, the locals quickly provided Danie's contact information to the CID agents, who promptly went to the security company compound and contacted the country manager. Although there wasn't a way to charge Danie with a crime, the company wasn't amused, and he lost a very good-paying job. He was quickly on the next plane out of the country with his name on a blacklist not to be hired for work in Iraq. He wouldn't be coming back. I don't know how much money he made with his little black-market car theft ring, but I doubt it was worth losing his job and getting his name on the naughty list.

CHAPTER 13

Travels with Casper

Very few Americans speak Arabic, and even fewer speak it well. Few Iraqis or Kurds speak English. When I was on the convoy security contract, the team's vehicles consisted of four up-armored F350 trucks with crew cabs. Each crew consisted of one American, who was both the driver and the vehicle commander, and three or four Kurdish shooters. That came down to four Americans for every 14 to 16 Kurds on each team.

I could barely communicate with my Kurdish crew members, but everyone knew their job, so it all worked out pretty well most of the time. But there were also many occasions when we had to interact with Iraqis, either at the facilities we were transporting the weapons and equipment to, or at checkpoints. Consequently, there was usually an interpreter assigned to each team. The company didn't trust local Iraqis, with good reason, so they elected to go a little more exotic when they sourced interpreters. They hired Lebanese Christians. The interpreter for my team spoke excellent English and rode shotgun with me. He went by the call sign Casper.

Casper was a former Lebanese Christian militiaman, so he had a lot of experience in city fighting during the Lebanese Civil War. Like many people in the Middle East, it was hard to tell his exact age, and to be honest I never asked. Since the Lebanese Civil War had officially ended well over 20 years previously, he had to be in his late 30s. He wasn't a big guy, maybe 5'7" and around 150 pounds, but he had presence. The kind of confident presence you radiate when you've faced death many times and come out of it alive.

Casper's front teeth were a different color from the rest. One day after we'd been on a few missions together, I asked him what the deal was. Anyone who has been in the military or in the kinds of situations we were in daily knows you can get pretty familiar with the guy next to you, so he didn't mind me asking.

He told me they were fake. He'd been captured by the Syrians during the fighting in Beirut when he was a 16-year-old militiaman. They'd smashed his front teeth out with a rifle butt when they took him prisoner. They'd had him and some other prisoners sitting on the floor in the second-floor hallway of a building on the Syrian side of the city. He convinced them he had to go to the bathroom badly, and since they were on the second floor, they let him go. They didn't send anyone in with him, so he escaped by jumping out of the second-story window and making his way back across the city into friendly territory. I asked him if his father had fought in the militia, too. He laughed and said no, his father made screen doors for people's houses.

Casper didn't have a dimmer switch. We stopped for lunch in a relatively safe area on the edge of a Coalition base one day. The local Iraqi truck drivers somehow sent someone off for hot food, and before long they were all sitting around in groups on the ground scooping up rice and lamb from tin platters with their fingers. We were eating MREs.

When it was time to go, we sent one of the Kurds to tell the drivers to mount up. He left his AK in the truck. We really should have known better, because Iraqi Arabs and Kurds don't like each other, but we didn't think him telling them it was time to get back on the road would be a problem. We were wrong.

When he didn't come back after 10 minutes, we went looking for him. We heard shouting and looked under one of the trailers and saw a cluster of feet on the other side. The Iraqi drivers had our Kurd surrounded and were yelling and pushing him around. Before any of us could say anything, Casper said he'd handle it. He drew his Glock from his vest and walked into the crowd. Like I said, Casper wasn't a big guy, but he went straight for the biggest Iraqi in the mob. He put the muzzle of the gun against the guy's head and started yelling at him in Arabic, banging the muzzle against the side of the guy's head with every word. The Iraqis broke in all directions to get back in their trucks. Casper holstered his pistol like nothing had happened and grinned at us. We all just looked at each other and shrugged. Just another day in Iraq.

I heard another story about Casper from several of the guys I worked with. I wasn't there, since it occurred just before I came on board with the company. It went like this.

The company occasionally ran short-term PSD missions for visiting expats who didn't have regular contracts for security services. People like journalists on short assignments and the occasional businessperson. I went on a couple of them myself. When the company was doing a PSD mission, they only used Americans and sometimes the Lebanese interpreters, but never the

Kurds. Casper and the three Americans in his vehicle were on a PSD mission somewhere in Baghdad when the team started taking fire. As always, the priority was to keep moving and get the clients out of the kill zone, so the team put the pedal down.

Unfortunately for the guys with Casper, their truck was immobilized and separated from the rest of the team. The guys bailed out of the truck and took refuge in a vacant building. They knew they couldn't stay there, but they weren't even sure where "there" was. All they knew was that they had to find a way to get out of the area. Casper, in true Casper fashion, went into action. He ducked out the back door of the building with the three Americans close behind him.

The door opened out into an alley that ran behind the building. After a few moments, a local came down the narrow street in a minivan. Casper stepped out into the alley and pointed a gun at the van, which stopped. He and the other guys piled in. Casper put his Glock up against the back of the driver's head and told him in Arabic to take them to BIAP, where the camp was. Blubbering in Arabic, the driver quickly complied and headed for BIAP.

Once they were close to the checkpoint, Casper told the guy to stop so they could get out. They didn't want to get too close to the checkpoint where the guards might see them holding a gun on a terrified local. There was no way to be sure how the guards would react ... probably not well. Before they got out Casper turned to the rest of the guys and said that since they'd put the poor Iraqi through quite an ordeal, they ought to do something nice for him to make up for it.

The guys all dug into their pockets and came up with a couple of hundred dollars which Casper gave the local. The story goes that the guy's eyes lit up and he tried to give them his phone number, telling them that if they ever needed his help again to just call him. They got out and walked the rest of the way to the checkpoint, and the Iraqi turned around and went on his way.

Is the story true, or just a great "No shit, there I was ..." war story? I wasn't there so I can't say for sure. I heard it from several different guys who were usually pretty reliable sources, and I saw the truck after it was recovered sitting in the salvage yard. It had numerous 30-caliber bullet holes in it, including some that damaged the engine enough that it wouldn't run. It also had 5.56mm bullet holes that had gone back to front through the passenger side mirror, apparently from one of the guys shooting back. Either way, it's a great story, and knowing Casper, one that isn't all that difficult to believe.

CHAPTER 14

A Buddhist in Iraq

When I first got to camp on my convoy escort contract, I and several other "new guys" were turned over to the admin guy for a few days to complete our paperwork, get our Common Access Cards (CACs), and get our gear issued. He was a young American (I'll call him Dave) with a perpetually sunny disposition. He was easy to talk to so, of course, we took advantage of that to find out everything we could about the camp and company.

In the course of talking to him, I found out he was a Buddhist monk. He had a regular haircut and dressed like everyone else, but he was a genuine monk who until recently had lived in a monastery somewhere in the United States. When I asked him what in the world he was doing in Iraq, he explained that there were two philosophical paths among the monks in his order. One group essentially lived in the monastery their entire lives, meditating and chanting to find their centers.

The other philosophy, the group he came from, believed that meditating and chanting were great, but at some point in their progression, they had to go on a journey to experience life and find themselves while doing so. He had felt that going to Iraq for a while was an excellent way to do that and since he had some administrative skills, he was able to get a job. He only planned to stay for a year, then he would return to his monastery for a time before moving on to another life experience. I never saw him without a smile, although there were times that seemed a little out of place.

Once, when he was telling us about the casualties the company had suffered over the past year, he told us about a Kurdish contractor who had a serious head wound from an IED. The force of the explosion had driven a splinter of steel through the side of his Level IIIA Kevlar helmet and into his head. These were the same helmets the military used, and I was aware of an incident in the Green Zone where an Iraqi had shot a soldier in the head with a 9mm pistol, and the helmet had saved his life. Unfortunately, the Kurd's helmet hadn't been enough to stop a splinter of steel traveling at several thousand feet per second.

His smile as he described the wound and the way the fluid from inside the guy's head seeped out through the crack in his skull seemed more than a little weird until I considered that Buddhists seldom get upset about anything. They just take every event as a part of life's progression from birth to death. It was all pretty esoteric to us, especially since we knew we would be out on the roads where an IED was a real possibility. Although I've read about Buddhism, it is the only close contact I've ever had with a genuine Buddhist monk and the fact that it occurred in Iraq is more than a little strange. But I suppose if you are on a philosophical journey to find your center, spending time in a war zone would be a good option. I guess in some ways that's what I was doing there, too.

CHAPTER 15

Pieter, the Beehives, and the Reporter

Pieter (not his real name) was a former South African special forces commando and a veteran of the border war with Angola. He always had a smile and was easy to get along with, but he definitely had a temper, too. He was younger than Dandre but had also been tasked with the dirty job of keeping order during the turbulent days as apartheid came to its inevitable and much-deserved end. Some of Pieter's mates told me a tale of his inventiveness back when he was a commando.

He had been ordered to clear all the demonstrators out of a city square in Johannesburg, the largest city in South Africa. He had been specifically ordered that no one was to be killed or even shot. While circling the site in a helicopter, he had wondered how he was ever going to get hundreds, if not thousands of demonstrators out of the square without violating his orders not to kill anyone. As the helicopter swung wide into the country to come around for another pass, he thought he saw a solution. Below them, he saw a farm with rows of beehives in a field.

He told the pilot to land and asked if he had any plastic refuse bags with him (I had to get that clarified to mean black plastic trash bags). They landed the helicopter and proceeded to put the large black trash bags over the tops of three of the hives, and then loaded them into the helicopter.

They took off and flew back to hover over the square full of people. Once over the square, they pushed each of the hives out of the chopper, changing their position a little bit between each one. The wooden hives hit the ground and shattered, releasing swarms of very agitated bees. The square was clear of people within minutes.

I asked Pieter about it later and he admitted it was true. He said he'd gotten a major butt-chewing from his commander, but that he'd had to admit that the tactic had worked and prevented a confrontation between the demonstrators and the security forces. And no one was shot.

I don't know how much truth is in the bee story, but it was definitely entertaining and something I could have seen Pieter doing. But like any alpha male, he also had his dark side. The security company where Pieter worked had a compound in the Green Zone. They had some extra rooms built up like a rough motel that they rented out to provide secure accommodation to people coming into the city for short-term assignments who didn't have anywhere else to stay. This included lone journalists on short assignments. One of these journalists had arrived at the compound one evening and hadn't been introduced to most of the team members stationed there. As part of their accommodation, they had access to a couple of soft-skinned SUVs they could use to drive around the Green Zone, which wasn't all that big.

Pieter came out of his trailer (the South Africans called them caravans) one morning to see someone he didn't know get into one of the company SUVs, so he went over to the vehicle to see who it was. I guess the journalist, like many journalists, thought he was clever and jokingly said he was just passing by and saw the vehicle sitting there and decided to borrow it. Pieter tried to clarify things, and the journalist persisted with the "joke." That was a mistake.

His patience exhausted, Pieter reached through the open driver's window, grabbed the guy by his shirt, dragged him out through the window, and slammed him against a wall. One of the other team members who knew that the journalist was staying there rushed over as the now terrified man desperately explained who he was and tried to apologize. Upon finding out the truth, Pieter released the guy and straightened his shirt, then apologized and told the journalist to enjoy his stay. You really do have to know when to joke and when to play it straight.

The Land of Not Quite Right

Iraqi society seems to thrive on chaos. There is very little order in any social or commercial interaction, at least as far as I, as an American, could see. For example, there is no real concept of patiently standing in service lines at places like airports or other businesses. More than once while standing in a line at the airport waiting for a boarding pass, a local would walk around the line and just step up to the counter in front of whoever was already there. It resulted in more than one shoving match when an angry expat objected to the local cutting line. Invariably, the local would look surprised that the expat was objecting to him butting in line. He just couldn't comprehend what the issue was. Trust me, I understand that different countries and cultures have different social mores and rules. But it was more than that.

The whole time I was in Iraq, I marveled at the fact that the people there could function on a daily basis. That cars and trucks would run, and there would be electricity in their homes. As it turned out, electricity was more unreliable than I realized when I first arrived in Iraq. Contractors brought in their own large generators, so we were insulated from the electrical power problems the locals had to deal with.

But in general, we often found ourselves shaking our heads at the implausible way the locals went about things. For example, one day on the road we saw a small pickup truck loaded with a stack of bales of straw or something, that had to be stacked at least eight or ten feet high. Perched on the very top of the bales were three children. I shuddered to think of what would happen if the truck swerved or stopped suddenly. We also couldn't wrap our heads around some of the social and cultural differences from what we were used to in America. It caused us to coin the term "The land of not quite right" to describe how we saw Iraq's daily functioning.

CHAPTER 16

OSHA and Extension Cords

Because US reconstruction contractors were on the government dime, they had to comply with US government regulations for workplace safety. Security companies weren't running construction projects, so we didn't worry about OSHA regulations, the US government Occupational Safety and Health Administration, but our employers generally did. They would bring in government-certified expat safety engineers to keep an eye on things and satisfy government contract requirements. This gave rise to all sorts of unresolvable issues between the safety engineers and the local workers. For example, OSHA regulations for construction workers call for steel-toe work boots. But the Iraqi working class essentially lives in flip flops, what we call shower shoes. Forcing them to wear work boots was impossible since, as far as I knew, there was no place to buy work boots in Iraq even if they could have gotten the locals to go for them, which they couldn't no matter how hard they tried. Since the reconstruction contractors had no recourse but to use local labor, it was an unresolvable issue, and seeing a bunch of Iraqis swinging picks and shovels while wearing shower shoes was a common sight.

One place the safety guys did have the ability to intervene was with the equipment the local cleaning staff used in the camps, extension cords in particular. Since most camps consisted of a collection of second-hand prefabs and trailers brought in from all over the place, the electrical outlets were not standardized. Three different trailers might have three different kinds of outlets. The same was true for some Iraqi houses and business buildings. That made it difficult to plug extension cords in. To get around this, the Iraqis would simply cut the plugs off the cords and strip a few inches of insulation off the ends of the two bare wires. That way they could just stick the bare wires into the outlet, which would work regardless of the plug configuration.

This put the safety engineers into a state of apoplexy. Their solution was to standardize all the wall outlets in the camp, collect all the old extension cords, and give the Iraqi cleaning staff shiny, new ones. They patiently explained the risk of electrocution and the importance of using the nice new extension cords with the plugs attached. Once the Iraqis nodded and said they understood, they handed out the new extension cords and went on their way. Problem solved. Within an hour the Iraqis had cut all the plugs off the new wires and gone back to the business as usual of sticking the two bare wires into the outlet.

CHAPTER 17

How to Change a Tire, Iraqi Style

Most Americans know how to use a jack to change a flat tire, especially if you grew up on a farm like I did. You must get the wheel up high enough to take the weight off the flat tire so you can take it off and get the new inflated tire on. One day as I walked through camp, I noticed three of our Iraqi maintenance guys clustered around a Toyota pickup truck with a flat tire on one front wheel. They had jacked it up by putting one of the little jacks that come with trucks under the front bumper and jacking it as high as it would go. The problem was that the wheel was still hanging low enough on the suspension that they couldn't get the flat tire off. The truck was sitting on uneven ground, and they had stacked rocks and blocks of wood up under the jack but still couldn't get it jacked up high enough. They were stacking more rocks to put a second, even more unstable jack under the bumper in the hopes of getting the wheel high enough to change the tire. Of course, even if they managed to get the old tire off, they would have had to jack the truck up even higher to get a new inflated tire back on.

It was none of my business, but it was just painful watching these guys, not to mention the fact that as unstable as it was there was a good chance the jack would tip over and the truck would fall on one of them, so I went over. I took the second jack from them and showed them that they should put the second jack under the suspension instead of the bumper and jack it up to lift the wheel off the ground. I watched for a minute until I was sure they had the idea, and then went on my way. When I came back through about 15 minutes later the truck was gone, so I knew they had succeeded. I also knew they could be taught if the solution seemed to make sense to them.

Some people I worked with thought Iraqis were stupid, but they are not. They really know how to get by with less, and they come up with some ingenious ways to get around problems that would leave some Americans scratching their heads. They just have a different outlook on things than we do. Add to that the fact that many of the locals hired by contractors for maintenance work had no background or skills in that kind of work. When the US shut down the Iraqi military and Baʿath party government, they put hundreds of thousands of people out of work who then took any job they could get, whether they knew how to do it or not. So it was no wonder that many times, they didn't have the experience or skills to do the things we would expect an American maintenance person to know how to do.

CHAPTER 18

Iraqi Plumbing

The term Iraqi plumbing should be considered an oxymoron. One of the first things you notice in any Iraqi bathroom is the smell. Most Iraqi drains I've seen don't use a U-bend or trap. In case you don't know what that is, it's the u-shaped piece of pipe in the drain under your sink. It traps a little pool of water in your drainpipe that creates a seal to prevent odors from the sewer from backing up into your sink. Most Iraqi plumbing I've seen is just a straight pipe going into the sewer that allows the wonderful smell of the sewer water to come right back up into your sink. This creates a delightful ambiance when you brush your teeth.

Anytime I lived in a villa on the local infrastructure, as opposed to a contractor camp, it wasn't long before the drains were overflowing, and the water pressure was barely a trickle. Most Iraqi bathrooms don't feature Western-style toilets. Instead, there is a porcelain-lined hole in the floor with two places to put your feet so you can squat over it. Instead of toilet paper, there is usually a small faucet that might have a short length of hose attached to it. Barring that, there is a stack of water bottles. I'll let you use your imagination as to how you clean up after using the bathroom. We always brought our own toilet paper, usually the little packets that come in MREs. Interestingly, the villas where the more affluent Iraqis had once lived had two sets of bathrooms. The nicer ones that the well-to-do residents used had Western-style toilets and toilet paper holders, while the ones the servants used had the Iraqi hole-in-the-floor toilets. I guess the rich Iraqis didn't like to squat either.

During one close protection gig, I worked where the DoD contracting authority had set up shop in a former Iraqi government building in the Green Zone. The plumbing there was especially inadequate. The building had actual Western-style toilet stalls and toilet paper rolls. The problem was that there wasn't enough water pressure to successfully flush the toilets, and even if they did flush, they quickly overflowed because the sewers were backed up. Putting toilet paper down the toilet only made the problem worse. So, each toilet stall had a trash can in it, and after cleaning up you would simply throw your used toilet paper in the trash can. Sanitary isn't a word I would apply to the arrangement. The plumbing system just wasn't capable of dealing with the sheer number of people working in the occupation administration.

The inadequacy of the Iraqi sewer system was evident in a stretch of secondary road near Radwaniyah just a little way off Route Irish that was covered by a large, but shallow pond of raw sewage. Signs in English on the road warned oncoming vehicles to slow down to prevent atomizing the sewage into the air, and for occupants to roll up their windows to avoid breathing it. The smell was delightful, especially if you were headed to or from the DFAC.

CHAPTER 19

Keeping the Power Flowing

Americans take electricity for granted. We have the occasional power failure, but for the most part, we always know the light will come on when we flip the switch. The same cannot be said for Iraq, before or after the invasion. The power grid was an astonishing composite of outdated and barely functioning power plants connected to an array of wiring that would make a bowl of Asian noodles look organized.

A main power line would run on poles down the street like in any other place. But connected to it in every haphazard direction and method imaginable would be literally hundreds of wires that ran off in all directions to people's houses. When a local wanted electricity for his home, he would simply connect a wire to his house, drag it out into the street, find something to stand or climb on, and then splice it into the main power line while the juice was on. I never understood why there weren't piles of electrocuted Iraqis lying in the streets, but they seemed to succeed most of the time. Of course, all those jury-rigged wires would quickly overwhelm the main circuit, and the power line would either burn up or fail at some source upstream.

Everyone who has seen articles or videos about the Iraq invasion has seen the pictures of the huge, crossed swords on the parade grounds in Baghdad. These things are massive and comprise the two arches at each end of the parade ground where Saddam liked to go and build up his ego by watching his army pass in review. When I got to Iraq in 2004, it was still the Wild West, and we could go anywhere we wanted to. My buddies and I wandered through the complex and even climbed up into one of the hands that held the swords. Saddam had a bedroom built into the lower level of the reviewing stand that had a massive, armored window that looked out onto the parade ground. I cut a square out of the bedroom carpet as a souvenir. Presumably, he and whatever adolescent sex toy he had procured that night would lay in the bed while his tanks paraded back and forth.

The parade ground had large banks of stadium lights so the fun could go on after dark. The lights were so powerful, and the power grid so inadequate, that half of Baghdad would experience either a brownout or complete power failure when parades were held at night. Saddam didn't mind it if the populace didn't have power, but if his lights didn't work, heads would roll.

One of my clients had contracts to help get the power plants around Baghdad back up to operating speed. One of these was the Dora Power Plant on the east bank of the Tigris River. It was in an exposed part of the city and was a target for the insurgents. A key aspect of any insurgency is to cause the people's trust and confidence in the government to deteriorate. Interrupting key services like electricity fits the bill nicely, so power plants and electrical substations were prime targets. I went to Dora with my employer and a security team, to provide security while they inspected the plant, and to evaluate the on-site security measures. It was right on the river and included a large tank farm for the fuel that was used to generate steam from the river water to turn the turbines. A single rocket or mortar round would be all it would take to burst the tanks and send blazing fuel into the plant. We kept a South African Mamba armored truck there to use as a mobile bunker in the event of a mortar attack. They were pretty tough and would have stopped anything but a direct hit. Plus, since it was mobile, it could be used to get the clients out of the area in the event of an attack that ruptured a fuel tank.

The chief American engineer on the client's team really knew his stuff. It was interesting walking around with him as he inspected the plant and explained how it worked and all the problems he was finding. Essentially, the place was held together with wire and hundred-mile-an-hour tape. When we got back to the control room and asked the Iraqi engineer on duty why everything was such a mess, he said it was simple. When Saddam was in control, if the power failed on any given shift, he would threaten to kill not only the engineer and crew on shift but their families as well. Consequently, they would make whatever jury-rigged repairs they had to just to keep it running until the next shift came on duty. Once the shift changed, dealing with the repairs was the next crew's problem. Nothing was ever repaired properly because that might mean taking the plant offline, so the jury-rigged repairs just added up over the years until they reached critical mass and things started failing.

CHAPTER 20

"But you said you wanted the left rear window to work"

Probably the single event that solidified my "land of not quite right" outlook involved a local auto mechanic who had a little shop near our camp. When I was working convoy escort, our camp was right off the edge of the runways on BIAP. One of the soft-skin sedans we used for PX runs needed the power window fixed, and our admin guy asked me if I would follow him over there to bring him back after he dropped it off. I was on a down day and just hanging around the camp, so I said sure. I went with him to talk to the mechanic and listened as he explained that he wanted him to fix the left rear power window so it would work. The local mechanic smiled and nodded, and we left.

It was finished that afternoon, so I took the admin guy back over to get it. I'd seen enough of Iraq by now that I decided it would be a good idea to test the window before we paid the guy. Sure enough, the left rear window worked just fine. Me, being me, I decided to test the other windows too, just to be sure. The right rear window no longer worked, although it had worked when we dropped the car off. We went to the mechanic and asked him what the deal was.

He looked genuinely surprised by our question. His response? "But you said you wanted the left rear window to work." He had taken the good window motor out of the right rear door and used it to replace the bad window motor in the left rear door. In his mind, he had done exactly what we asked him to do.

We just looked at each other for a moment, and then the admin guy very slowly explained to the mechanic that we needed all the windows to work. And thus, the term "The land of not quite right" was born. I never did find out what the final outcome was since I was back on mission rotation the next day and it wasn't my problem anyway.

CHAPTER 21

Do Not Embarrass Me!

One day when I was working as a country security manager, I was called to the front gate of our client's camp in the Green Zone. A country security manager is essentially responsible for all aspects of security for their employer for the entire country. That meant that no matter how big or small a problem was, it was ultimately my responsibility so if I was available the other security personnel would often refer the situation to me. When I arrived, the guards presented an Iraqi man who wanted access to the camp. The man said he was the husband of one of our local housekeepers who did work like cleaning the hooches (living quarters) and office buildings. He explained that he was there to work in her place for a few days. When we asked where his wife was and why she couldn't come to work herself, he explained that she had embarrassed him in public last night. As a result, when he got her home, he punished her by beating her severely enough that she would not be able to come to work for a few days.

The other American security guy and I listening to the story were dumbstruck for a few moments. We just stared at him, not knowing quite what to say. Our first inclination was to punch the guy's lights out for beating his wife. But since we were nice guys, and that wouldn't have been nice, we had the interpreter explain to him that he was a dirtbag for beating his wife and that it was impossible for him to work in her place because he wasn't employed by the company and he hadn't been cleared to enter the compound. He looked downcast and tried to argue that his family needed the money she would lose by not working. At that point, we lost our cool and told him that it would be his fault and not his wife's if they were short on money that week and to get lost before we showed him what a beating was.

The head Iraqi housekeeper was standing there dressed in a traditional *jilbab*, an Islamic woman's cloak not quite as enveloping a *chador* or *burqa* but still covering the entire body. She spoke good English and had heard both sides of the conversation. After the man had left, she looked at us and said she didn't understand why we were so upset. If the man's wife had embarrassed him, she deserved to be beaten. Once again, we were speechless. It just made no sense to us that another woman would think it was okay for the guy to beat his wife so badly that she couldn't even go to work. But that was just the way things were in Iraq.

CHAPTER 22

Let's Pretend for a Minute That I Know What I'm Talking About

The Coalition employed many thousands of Iraqis to do all sorts of work during the occupation. One of the many jobs they did was loading trucks at the Abu Ghraib warehouse complex. The facility was overseen by the US Marine Corps, but the work was done by Iraqis supervised by civilian contractors. The place probably had an official name, but we just called it Abu Ghraib because that's where it was located.

We would show up at our appointed time in the morning to pick up our convoy but would sit there for hours while the facility staff tried to get the trucks loaded in some semblance of order. Some of the trucks had only one destination, so it didn't matter how the material was loaded onto them. However, others had to make multiple stops to drop off material for various Iraqi security forces. Logic would dictate that the material for the closest drop-off would be loaded last so it would be at the back of the truck and easy to unload. But the Iraqis had no such concept of organization and generally just loaded everything in random order. That meant that the entire truck would have to be unloaded at its first destination so that everything for that site could be found. Then everything not intended for that site had to be loaded back onto the truck for its next stop.

Needless to say, this slowed down the process considerably, resulting in much longer days for us and the truck drivers. The expat contractors at the distribution center tried their best to get the Iraqis to follow basic load plans and load everything in the proper order. Unfortunately, that seemed beyond them, and the contractors had to explain over and over what needed to be done. Being bored while we waited for the convoy to be ready to pull out, the exchanges between the contractors and the Iraqi workers were a source of entertainment as we waited. One of the civilians was particularly colorful in his style and loudly said, "Let's pretend for a minute that I know what I'm talking about," to the Iraqi foreman as he tried for the third time to get the truck loaded with the items for the first stop at the back of the truck. We all burst out laughing at the look on the Iraqi guy's face at that request. To us, it was just one more indicator that Iraq truly was the land of not quite right. It wasn't that Iraqis were stupid; they weren't. They just had a different way of approaching things.

CHAPTER 23

There is No EPA in Iraq

One of the details about war that many people don't think about is sanitation. There were tens of thousands of extra people suddenly thrown into a country with rudimentary sewage systems. Besides that, many of those extra people, both soldiers and contractors, lived in temporary camps that sprung up in a matter of days and were never hooked up to any kind of local sewer system, even if there was one. And that's not to mention people in places where there was nowhere to go to the bathroom. All those people had to relieve themselves somewhere.

There were two solutions to the problem. In the temporary camps and compounds where prefabricated quarters were brought in, the folks building the camp set up a whole new sewer system for the camp, along with running water and electricity. Those systems had their own sewage tanks for all of those toilets and sinks to drain into. The other solution for the really temporary sites, like the fuel points set up on the major convoy routes, was porta-potties. There were hundreds of thousands of blue porta-potties all over the country. In fact, some service contractors made millions of dollars doing nothing but renting porta-potties to the US government.

All that raw sewage had to go somewhere. All US government agencies, as well as contractors, must comply with the US Environmental Protection Agency (EPA) regulations for the disposal of sewage. So, all contractors and the military hired local Iraqi companies to come and pump out the tanks, empty the porta-potties, and take the effluent away for proper disposal. This brings me to our camp on the water pumping station construction site.

The camp had a sewage system that carried wastewater from all the living quarters and office bathrooms into a big tank. An Iraqi truck would come every few days to empty the tank. The site sat right on the bank of the Euphrates River, which is pretty big and is a lifeline for the region. You would see the locals out on the river in the mornings fishing from small boats. They would stand up in the boat and cast their nets out over the water the same way they had been doing it for centuries. It looked almost biblical.

I was up in the guard tower one day just as the truck finished pumping the wastewater tank and left the compound. I watched as it drove up the road running along the river until it got to a point about 500 yards from the gate. Then, the driver pulled over and backed the truck up to the river. As I watched, the driver got out, went around to the back of the truck, and opened the drain valve, dumping the entire load into the river.

I watched in horror as the raw sewage poured out of the tank and into the water. The entire scene was made worse by the fact that there were several Iraqis fishing from small boats just a few yards downriver from where the truck was emptying. They just kept throwing their nets out into the water and pulling them in with a few fish in them without so much as a glance at the truck dumping hundreds of gallons of raw sewage into the water upstream. There was such a contrast between the two vistas. On the one hand, you had this peaceful scene of the local people fishing on the wide, quiet river. And on the other hand, you had this nasty, dirty truck dumping raw sewage into the water where the fish these people were going to eat lived. Our food was all brought in by truck, and we drank only bottled water, so it wasn't going to affect us too much, but it still sickened me.

It got even worse a week later. Our British liaison officer arranged a meeting for the project managers and me with the commanding general of the Iraqi 13th Infantry Division since they had responsibility for the security of the region. We would be going to his headquarters, and it would be a luncheon meeting. When we got there the general's servants were setting food and plates out on a large table; they brought out all sorts of delicious-looking Arabic dishes. The usual lamb and rice, along with several kinds of bread and hummus dips. And the centerpiece of the meal was several large fish. They were very artistically presented, skewered up through their bodies, and stood up on their tails in a very convincing pose as if they were jumping out of the water. The general said something to his flunky in Arabic, and the man turned to us with a big smile and told us the fish was very fresh, just having been caught this morning. I pasted a smile on my face and nodded in approval and appreciation of the honor he was doing us.

Fortunately, the meal was served buffet style in the general's large office, so we could pick the foods we wanted. I went for rice, lamb, bread, and some hummus, steering well clear of the beautiful fish. At one point I managed to nudge one of the other contractors and warn him not to eat the fish, but several others who did all seemed to survive so I guess it wasn't too dangerous to eat. But, survive or not, there was no way I was touching the fish after watching that truck dump raw sewage into the river.

Just Like the Wild Geese

Even though private security contractors continually maintain that we are not mercenaries, there are some decidedly mercenary-like aspects to the work. One of them is getting screwed over by your employer.

The Wild Geese is a 1978 movie about mercenaries in Africa hired to rescue a deposed African politician. They are betrayed by their employer, left on their own in hostile territory, and forced to find their own way home. Private security contractors can at times unfortunately find themselves in a similar, if not quite so dire situation.

CHAPTER 24

Abandoned

In the fall of 2004, the company I had my first contract with fell on hard times. They had lost their contract with the DoD reconstruction contractor they were paid to provide security for. It wasn't really surprising, since even we could see that they were not meeting the obligations of their contract. It wasn't that we weren't providing good security and protection to the American engineers and construction managers we were escorted around Iraq: we were. We were doing our job, and several of our teammates had been wounded while doing it.

The problem was that the owners' goal of making a lot of money fast meant they were doing everything on a shoestring. The contract called for us to be in up-armored SUVs, but we were still running around in soft-skin vehicles. The contract also called for us to wear uniforms, so we would present a professional appearance. But we were all wearing whatever clothes we had brought with us or picked up at the PX. Some of us were wearing khaki 5.11s, while other guys were in jeans and T-shirts. Even our load-bearing equipment (LBE) was whatever we'd obtained for ourselves. The only gear the company provided was plate carriers, weapons, and radios.

The company owners were an American and a Brit, and the company had been formed and registered in Great Britain the year before to cash in on the Iraq security gold rush. The owners lived at the villa the company maintained at $20,000 a month in the Mansour district of Baghdad. When they lost the contract, they promoted one of the senior team leaders to country manager and sent him over to talk to us at the team house next to Radwaniyah so they wouldn't have to face us themselves. He assured everyone that the company would take care of us and that they were actively looking at new contracts. He finished by telling us to all take a few days off and punctuated it by having a couple of pallets of beer delivered to the main house. There were around 40

Americans and the same number of Nepalese team members, and everyone proceeded to get drunk and not worry about tomorrow.

But guys soon began to disappear. They would be sitting around talking with everyone the night before, and then they and their gear would be gone in the morning. Occasionally their friends would tell us they had found a new contract someplace. A couple of days later the company started sending guys home. Another of the senior team leaders came to tell me and my roommate that we and a few other guys were going home because the company didn't have a new contract yet and they couldn't afford to pay us to just sit around. That was fine with me since they would be paying for my airline ticket, and I didn't have any faith they would actually find a new contract anyway.

As it turned out, they never did. About a week after I was safely back in the States and looking for a new gig, a couple of the guys who were still in Iraq emailed to tell me the two owners had just disappeared. They got on a plane and flew out of Iraq without telling anyone, leaving everyone sitting high and dry in the team house and the villa.

The pay had always been a little sporadic. We got paid every month, but you never knew when it was going to show up in your account. When I went out, they owed me a couple of weeks' pay, about $5,000. I never got the money, but I was one of the lucky ones. At least I got a flight out on their dime.

The guys they left behind in Iraq didn't even find out the owners were gone for a few days. Once they found out, there was nothing they could do. The company worked through an office in England somewhere, and it just disappeared after the owners did. The guys sat around the team house and relied on their CAC cards to eat at the DFAC, so at least they weren't going to starve to death. But they weren't getting paid either, and one of my friends later told me he was out around $25,000 by the time he finally decided they were never going to pay him.

The Americans could at least run around to other security companies and try to find another gig. There were a lot of private security companies working in Iraq, and they were always hiring contractors. But it was far from a sure thing.

A month later I was back in Iraq with a new contract, this time with a well-known and established company. One day, several of the guys from my old contract showed up at our camp on BIAP trying to sell a couple of the Suburbans, along with AKs and ammunition to get money for tickets home. When my previous employers had bailed on everyone, they had just left everything sitting in Iraq, weapons, equipment, vehicles, and people. We used M4s instead of AKs so we couldn't do much for them there. But we were a little short on 9mm, so I picked up a few hundred rounds for my team just to help them out. As far as I know, the Americans all eventually got new gigs or at least tickets home. I saw many of them later in Iraq; it was a small community.

If the Americans had options open to them, the same couldn't be said for the Nepalese. At one point there were almost 70,000 third-country nationals (TCNs) working in Iraq, around 12,000 of whom were doing security work. They were recruited en masse in their home countries and brought into Iraq as groups with a specific contractor. For the Nepalis my former employer left behind, going around and finding a new job was nearly impossible. And since all their pay, which was much lower than that paid to American and British expats, had gone home to support their families, they had no money to get tickets home.

Their other problem was that after 12 Nepalese were kidnapped and murdered by Iraqi insurgents in 2004, Nepal banned its citizens from traveling to and working in Iraq. The Nepalese I had worked with were afraid that if they went home, they wouldn't be able to come back to Iraq on a new contract. So, they shuttled around the bases trying to find someone, anyone, who would give them a job. It was a shoddy way to treat guys who had been an integral part of our teams and had risked their lives next to us. I have no idea how they all finally came out, since over time I lost track of all but one of them, and his story had a very different ending.

Life on the Road

It may sound a little clichéd to say Iraq was the Wild West back in August 2004, but it really is the best way to describe the situation. After the invasion had officially ended, Paul Bremmer, who was assigned by the United States to head the Coalition Provisional Authority (CPA), issued Coalition Provisional Authority Order Number 2: Dissolution of Entities. This dissolved all Iraqi security forces. That included the military and the police leaving the country completely under the authority of the Coalition military.

In hindsight, this was a bad idea since it left the country in disorder with no police or security forces. Plus, all those former military men had to go somewhere. Many of them just melted into civilian unemployment and took their weapons with them where they served as a convenient manpower pool for the insurgents and militias. Others, especially the hard-line Saddam supporters, along with those who saw the United States as illegal occupiers of their country, went straight into the insurgency and formed the bands of mujahideen the US fought for years. Terrorist groups like Al Qaida quickly moved in to support the mujahideen with equipment and training to further their own ideology of hatred and murder.

Added to that was the fact that there was absolutely no order in the country. No law enforcement, no functional government, and certainly no one patrolling the roads except for Coalition military units, and they weren't there to enforce civilian laws. It was pretty much anarchy bordering on chaos.

On March 31, 2004, the Fallujah Blackwater ambush incident occurred. Iraqi insurgents ambushed a convoy escorted by four American contractors working for Blackwater USA, the best-known private security company in the United States. They were escorting trucks loaded with kitchen equipment destined for a catering company working on a US base, hardly a sensitive or high-priority cargo. The Blackwater guys were armed with small arms but riding in soft-skinned Pajero

SUVs. They did not have an adequate number of people to provide security around their vehicles. In short, they never stood a chance.

They were stationary, sitting in a traffic jam when armed Iraqis walked up to their vehicles and executed them. They were pulled from their bullet-riddled vehicles, and their mutilated corpses were burned and dragged through the city streets of Fallujah before being hung from a bridge. Photos of Iraqis posing with the burnt bodies were released on the internet for everyone to see. Those images were still fresh in our minds as I joined my team and we hit the roads five months later. We were determined to do our jobs and not end up like those Blackwater guys did.

CHAPTER 25

On Our Own

We quickly realized we were on our own when we went outside the wire. We were considered Coalition Forces by the military. Our CAC cards gave us access to all the military facilities like the DFAC, PX, and medical care. In a later contract, I even had a special access card to the US Embassy that authorized me to carry a gun in the embassy buildings and compound. However, there were no military escorts whatsoever for PSD teams, and only occasional escorts for convoy security, depending on what we were escorting. Contractors in Iraq eventually formed a working group and set up an operation center in the Green Zone to coordinate missions and develop a formal response mechanism when a contractor team was attacked, but that was still many months away when I started working.

In the early days, there were PSD teams and escorted convoys running all over the country on their own. There was no coordination, and no one outside their own operations room knew where they were or where they were going. It was dangerous and we knew it. IEDs were less common in late 2004 and early 2005 than they would become later, but they still existed. Ambushes from the roadside or other vehicles were common, and the specter of a VBIED (vehicle-borne improvised explosive device), commonly called a car bomb, was always present. The bad guys would convince a suicide driver that he would be a martyr and get his 72 virgins in Paradise if he drove a car loaded with explosives into a passing convoy and blew himself up, as long as he took some Americans with him.

The standard procedure when a private security vehicle was immobilized was to abandon it, usually after setting it on fire so the bad guys couldn't recover it or get anything useful from it. You sure couldn't leave three or four guys sitting by the roadside. Likewise, nobody was keen on the idea of trying to go back and recover a damaged vehicle because it would make the perfect bait for an ambush. All the bad guys would have to do is wait in hiding to shoot up the recovery team, or better yet, load the damaged vehicle up with explosives and wait for the team to start recovery before detonating it so most were never recovered. We regularly came upon destroyed SUVs by the roadside, sometimes while they were still burning. It was an eerie sight, and it always made us bump our awareness up another level.

In the early months of the occupation, if a team was stuck because all their vehicles were disabled or they had severely wounded people to care for, getting help was a long process. The team would radio or call back to their operations center and give a sit rep. The people at the ops center would try to contact the Coalition military to get some help out to the team. It would usually take a while to find the right military person and then determine what assets were in the area and who had authority over them. Once that was determined, the people with authority would have to contact those they had in the area and try to get them moving in the right direction. The whole process could take a long time. In the meantime, the stranded team might be sitting there surrounded by Iraqis who were possibly or overtly hostile. The wounded would be suffering, and the team might be taking fire.

This was always on our minds every time we went outside the wire on a mission. Consequently, we knew we were largely on our own, and we took whatever action we could to avoid becoming bogged down to the point where we would end up like those Blackwater guys had. Nobody wanted their family to see a video of them being beheaded online.

CHAPTER 26

A Deadly Environment

Most people don't realize how built-up Iraq is, at least in the Baghdad metropolitan area. The highway net from Sadr City east of Baghdad out to Abu Ghraib west of Baghdad, and quite a way north and south, is a lot like any urban highway system in the US. Lots of divided highways with typical overpasses and entrance ramps. In the cities, many roads and streets are divided by grassy medians or cement curbs. There's not much in the way of traffic signals and no one pays any attention to them if there are any. Traffic is chaotic, and everyone crowds each other to get ahead. All the drivers were male, which isn't necessarily a good thing in itself. There may have been women drivers, but I don't recall ever seeing a woman driving a vehicle. There were too many cultural taboos against it.

The main highways going north and south, and east and west through the country are like interstate highways in the US, with overpasses and entry ramps in some places and unlimited access from side roads in others. Some of the overpasses out in the desert have ramps but don't connect to any roads. I guess Saddam had them built when the highways were constructed to allow for future expansion of the highway network that never happened.

The thing to keep in mind about a PSD team is that all you have is two team vehicles and the client vehicle with eight or nine team members and three or fewer clients. When doing convoy escort, you have three or four trucks per team with a total of 12 to 16 team members spread out for the length of a convoy of anywhere from three to six tractor-trailers. If the convoy is any bigger than that you usually add another team to the escort. In both cases, the whole time you are en route, you are surrounded by scores or even hundreds of Iraqis. In an insurgency, what the military calls asymmetrical warfare, you have no way of knowing how many of the people around you are insurgents who may attack you at any moment, or are acting as spotters for ambush teams. Security teams were being attacked by IEDs and insurgents armed with AKs, and being stopped at roadblocks to immobilize them so they could be killed or kidnapped. You were completely on your own. Calling for backup was like calling 911 in the US: help might come but there was no way to know how long it would take or if it would get there in time. After my first contract with the fly-by-night company, all the vehicles I was in on subsequent contracts had "panic buttons" that sent out a signal if you were attacked, either manually or automatically if the unit sensed an explosion or the impact of a crash. But even that couldn't guarantee responders would get there in time to help.

The only defense was to keep moving and not get bogged down. That meant PSD teams moved fast and didn't stop for anything. It was a lot more difficult with a convoy because you had to stay with the trucks, so convoy escorts had to rely on keeping other vehicles as far away from the convoy as possible. This often meant putting their vehicle between the trucks and anything that looked like a threat. If the potential threat was just some hapless Iraqi who wasn't situationally aware enough to see he was getting close to a convoy, all you had to do was intimidate him to back off. If it was a bad guy with the intent to shoot at you or detonate a car bomb, violence would ensue.

Just because you weren't the intended target of an IED or VBIED didn't mean you couldn't get caught in the fallout from one. More than once, we saw an explosion a little way ahead or behind us, or one just off the edge of the road but far enough away not to seriously affect us. Whether it was targeted at someone else, or it was intended for us but missed, wouldn't matter if we were caught in the explosion. We saw that on more than one occasion when insurgents didn't care about collateral damage and locals were injured in explosions.

At least twice that I can recall, we came along just after a VBIED had detonated. The first one was in the lanes going in the opposite direction on an expressway. It was a real mess, with bits and pieces of cars and debris scattered everywhere. There were bodies on the road and locals running around trying to tend to them. I didn't see anything that looked like military vehicles so apparently it hadn't targeted a US convoy. No idea what they were after. It could have been targeting Iraqi police, or it could have been a VBIED that detonated accidentally before it got to wherever it was supposed to go off. That sort of thing happened every so often.

The second time was at an Iraqi police checkpoint. It had gone off long enough before we got there that there was no smoke in the air and traffic was moving. Damaged police pickup trucks were sitting around, but there were no bodies still in sight. The Iraqi police were all just standing around with shocked looks on their faces. I felt sorry for the guys. I understood how they felt having been through a couple of IEDs by then myself. Still, the adage of better them than us applied, and we were glad we hadn't been through a little earlier and been caught in the blast.

CHAPTER 27

Not Your Average Road Trip

The hazards of the roads in Iraq went beyond the threat of direct enemy action. There were plenty of risks to negotiate from the moment you got on the road until the moment you reached wherever you were going. There was no such thing as an average run, and even the relatively uneventful trips had plenty of problems to overcome.

The expressways were usually in pretty good condition, but many of the back roads through the desert were crumbling and full of potholes. Bridges were another matter. Some of the main highway bridges had been destroyed by American airstrikes during the invasion, which meant finding either an alternate route or a way to bypass the bridge. That worked fine if it was a bridge over a draw or a railway cut, but waterways were more problematic. Other bridges were being damaged by the insurgents. They either weren't very good at it, or they didn't have enough explosives to do the job right, because they usually just blew a hole in the roadway. The Army overcame these by throwing an armored vehicle launched bridge (AVLB) over the damaged portion. I'd driven plenty of tanks over them when I was in the Army, but they could be a bit disconcerting if you weren't used to them since they were single-lane, usually with no side rails of any kind. They slowed traffic down, but since they were designed for tanks, they were plenty wide enough to get a large truck across.

Fuel was always a concern. The F350 trucks we used for convoy escort had big V8 gasoline engines and 40-gallon fuel tanks. The Suburbans had smaller tanks but didn't use as much fuel. There were no Sheetz or 7-11s handy, and you couldn't just stop at some Iraqi gas station, so we had to calculate fuel usage on the longer runs and try to arrange routes to hit Army fuel points. Fortunately, being DoD contractors, we could use the fuel points just by providing a contract number. Nobody carried extra cans of fuel since nobody wanted them on the outside of their vehicle if it was being shot at. Shooting a hole in a can, and then hitting the spilled gasoline with a tracer round, would be an easy way to set a vehicle on fire.

Another real hazard was encountering friendly military patrols and convoys. Our vehicles didn't look much like local vehicles, but they were still civilian vehicles and not obviously military. That meant that we had to exercise caution when we came up on military patrols or convoys. We didn't dare to just come up fast behind one and zip by. They didn't let anything do that to them any more than we let it happen to us. And they had bigger guns. I once had a USMC LAV, an eight-wheeled light armored vehicle armed with an autocannon and a machine gun, swing the turret around and point its 25mm Bushmaster chain gun at us. Not good.

If they were going slow and we wanted to pass them, we had to come up very carefully and make sure they identified us as Americans, and then signal for permission to go past them. Then the military vehicle would radio the convoy commander up at the front of the convoy and wait for his or her ruling. If they signaled to us that we could go past, we would. Otherwise, we followed them. There is no such thing as friendly fire.

Roadblocks and checkpoints were not a problem if they were manned by Americans. Anything manned by Iraqis was another matter altogether. There had been several incidents of contractors being abducted at unauthorized roadblocks by bad guys dressed as Iraqi security troops. They may have even been actual security troops who'd turned. Either way, it didn't end well for the contractors. If we came across one, we would stop a good way back from it and see if we could verify whether it was legitimate by contacting our operations room. If we couldn't verify it, we would either find a way around it or blow through it without stopping. We probably pissed some people off that way, but no one ever shot at us. Either they were all legit, or the fact that we were armed and being cagey about it told them we weren't a soft target. Whatever the case, we got past them.

CHAPTER 28

A Law unto Ourselves

The realization that we were on our own made it clear to us that our best chance of survival, and that of our clients when doing PSD and the truckers when escorting convoys, was to take as much control as possible in any given situation. Since there was no law and order out there on the road, we essentially became a law unto ourselves. That doesn't mean we went around shooting things up or harming civilians, it just meant that we had to make split-second decisions on a daily basis, and the foundation of those decisions was to accomplish every mission and survive it.

Some PSD teams prefer to go with a low-profile approach. That means they use sedans instead of SUVs so they blend in better and aren't so obvious as a PSD team. That's a great approach until you run up against a roadblock or get stuck in traffic and someone recognizes who and what you are. Sedans have low ground clearance, making it difficult to jump curbs or veer off the road to go around a roadblock. That problem is made even worse if the sedan has an extra few thousand pounds of armor built into it. In a situation like that you are suddenly immobilized with no avenue of escape, making you a stationary target.

All the PSD teams I worked on or with preferred the brute force approach made possible by using SUVs. In a country like Iraq, where most of the population drives small cars the size of a Toyota Corolla or a Prius, the size and weight of an armored Excursion or up-armored Suburban allowed you to bully other cars out of the way and gave you the option to jump a curb, go off-road, or even plow through a roadblock. Options we used whenever we had to.

There were many times we had to jump a center median to change direction on a divided city street or road to get around congested traffic or other problems. There were also times that we simply crossed the median, and then kept going in our original direction down the other side of the road running against the traffic flow. We did our best to run down the shoulder of the road and not down the middle of the street to give the oncoming Iraqis plenty of room. We didn't run them off the road, at least not in those circumstances. We didn't have to, since any driver seeing a Suburban coming at them on the wrong side of the road gave us plenty of room.

Changing direction by making a U-turn or turning left across traffic created danger points because the team, and the clients, could easily get stopped by oncoming traffic and placed in a vulnerable position for an ambush. We handled this by the simple expedient of the lead vehicle turning left and stopping in the middle of the lane to block the road to oncoming traffic. If any oncoming car seemed unwilling to stop or made a move that indicated they were going to veer around the stopped SUV, and therefore be in a position to threaten the client vehicle, the team members on that side of the vehicle discouraged them by pointing their AKs or M4s at them until they stopped. No one on any team I was on or with ever fired a shot in those circumstances, as the simple threat of them doing so always stopped the oncoming drivers. Once the client and trail vehicles had safely made the turn, the stopped vehicle caught up with them and took its place at the front of the convoy. I'm sure the Iraqi drivers didn't appreciate this; I know I wouldn't. But we were in constant hypervigilance mode and all too aware of the potential for sudden death on the roads. It happened with depressing regularity.

In one case, a PSD team from another company picked up their client at BIAP to bring him to Baghdad. The team made the trip from BIAP toward Baghdad on what the Iraqis called Airport Street or the Qadisaya Expressway, and what the Coalition called Route Irish. It was known as "the most dangerous seven miles of road in the world" for a good reason. They were crossing an overpass and were almost at the Green Zone entry checkpoint (ECP) when an oncoming car full of explosives veered across the divider and exploded next to the vehicle the client was riding in. The explosion threw the client's vehicle off the overpass in a ball of fire. It happened so fast that there was nothing the rest of the team could do. One moment it was a routine airport run, and the next the vehicle the client had been riding in was on its roof on the road below the overpass burning. People could hear small arms ammunition in the burning vehicle cooking off in the fire. Two PSD team members and the client were killed instantly. It was the client's first trip to Iraq, and he had been in the country for less than two hours.

We did everything we could to be prepared for anything. That included acquiring whatever we could to increase our firepower, even if we weren't supposed to have it. The Coalition had guidelines for how contractors could be armed. Small arms and medium machine guns like M240s and PKMs were okay, but we weren't authorized anything larger like a .50 caliber heavy machine gun. A South African we knew had a Russian 12.7 at one time, but the Army came and confiscated it from him. Still, we managed to come up with more easily concealed weapons like frag and white phosphorus grenades, which were good for setting a disabled vehicle on fire. A couple of the convoy teams even had RPGs in case they got bogged down in a firefight after the insurgents disabled a truck.

CHAPTER 29

Crash!

The need for speed among PSD teams didn't always work out well. Iraqi drivers are erratic and that combined with high speeds isn't always a good mix. We found that out the hard way one afternoon.

The first company I worked for had teams located all over Iraq to meet the needs of our client. One of those places was Firebase Laramore-Matthews, a tiny base located on a former Iraqi airbase on the other side of the expressway from Bayji. We just called the place K2, but I never did know why. Our client didn't have any projects there, it was just a little camp for them to stage out of if they had to travel to northern Iraq. Aside from an Army fuel point and some artillery units, there wasn't much there, just a DFAC, a PX, and a small gym. We lived in trailers next to the old runway. Because it was boring, we rotated teams between Baghdad and K2 every few months. It was my team's turn to go there.

The trip there from Baghdad was technically an administrative move since we wouldn't have a client with us. The company had a bizarre policy of using our Iraqi employees as drivers for administrative moves. They reasoned that the locals were more used to Iraqi traffic, and since it was an administrative move there wouldn't be any need for professional PSD driving skills. I'm not sure how they reasoned that, since we were still obviously a team of Americans in Suburbans, but they did. As it turned out, the Iraqis driving our Suburbans were just as bad as every other Iraqi driver on the road.

The trip was up Iraqi Route 1, which if I recall correctly, was codenamed Route Jackson. I was in the second seat behind the driver and tasked with watching/shooting out the left rear window. The guy next to me in the back seat had folded the seat down and was facing backward to watch the road to the rear of us. He was armed with an old British Sterling submachine gun he had scrounged up somewhere. The 9mm Sterling was an archaic gun that fired from an open bolt. That made it prone to going off accidentally. The back section of the Suburban was loaded with our gear in packs and black plastic footlockers we got at the PX.

Our Iraqi driver was tooling along at around 75mph. We were somewhere just south of Taji when a large Iraqi truck loaded to the gills with big silver tins of cooking oil veered over into our lane in front of us. Our driver didn't even attempt to miss it and just plowed into the rear end. I remember looking around as I heard the team leader in the front seat yell just in time to see us hit the truck. Several big tins of oil flew off the back of the truck and hit the hood and windshield of our vehicle.

Nobody was wearing seat belts since they made it impossible to turn and move around inside the vehicle. My face slammed forward into the back of the driver's headrest. I recall my face hitting the headrest twice, the second time was probably when we went through the guardrail.

Everything seems to slow down during a crash, or most other traumatic experiences, and I distinctly remember turning my head in time to see the footlockers in the back flying forward toward us. We always traveled with a round in the chamber, and I remember thinking that I hoped the guy with the Sterling had it pointed somewhere besides at me as our gear came crashing forward during the wreck. I was able to duck, but a footlocker hit him square in the face just before we jolted to a halt.

It was a good thing there were guardrails since the accident happened on top of an overpass that crossed a dry wadi in the desert. The SUV ended up with the front end hanging off the side of the bridge. We had been the first vehicle and our second SUV pulled up and stopped. We were all stumbling out of the wreck and taking up a perimeter when a patrol of American HUMVEEs stopped to ask if we needed assistance. Some Iraqis also stopped and came running back toward us, probably just to help, but we all leveled our AKs at them and they stopped. We had no idea what their intentions were, or if the truck had been part of a plan to stop us to facilitate an attack. It seems paranoid, I know, but that sort of thing had happened before.

Our reaction and training were good. We had all the gear transferred and everyone crammed into the second SUV and were on our way in six minutes. I had to hold one of my footlockers on my lap or we would have had to leave it behind because there was no room for it anywhere else. We just left the wrecked Suburban there, hanging off the edge of the bridge.

We did a verbal check of how everyone was doing as we headed for the nearest American military base to get medical treatment. I believe it was Camp Cook at Taji, but that was a while ago and we were all pretty rattled so I could be mistaken. Surprisingly, other than some cuts and bruises, we were all in pretty good shape except the guy with the Sterling. He had a concussion from the footlocker hitting him in the head, so we left him there to get medevaced back to Baghdad. We all survived, and I didn't get shot, so I put the whole experience in the win column.

Our Iraqi driver hadn't even tried to miss the truck, he'd just driven straight into the rear end. I told the team leader I wouldn't ride with an Iraqi driver again. I didn't have to, since that was the last time we ever let one drive a team anywhere, even on an administrative move.

CHAPTER 30

Traffic Control Convoy Style

PSD teams survive by moving as fast as they can and not standing still if they can avoid it. When I was working PSD, we normally traveled at 65–75mph when on the open highway. That made it more difficult for spotters and insurgents to accurately target our vehicles with IEDs or small arms fire. We couldn't go that fast in built-up areas, so we were especially vigilant and nervous when moving at lower speeds. If an attack occurs, the team does whatever it must to get the client out of the kill zone, even if that means abandoning a disabled vehicle.

Of course, that's all different when you are escorting convoys. The average speed of a convoy was somewhere around 30mph, although we could occasionally get them up to 50mph on the open highway. If a truck broke down or became disabled, the entire convoy had to stop and protect it. We couldn't just leave a truck loaded with weapons or military equipment sitting there unprotected for the insurgents to loot, not to mention a driver. The driver would not abandon his truck if it broke down, since it was an expensive vehicle and his livelihood. But the insurgents had no problem killing drivers who were working for the Americans. And you couldn't leave a single escort vehicle behind on its own to guard a disabled truck while the rest of the convoy escorts went with the convoy, because they would be easily overwhelmed if insurgents showed up. The only option left was to call for help while the entire team circled the wagons in a defensive posture until it arrived. This made convoys extremely vulnerable to attack and escorting them was incredibly dangerous.

Attacks were common, usually occurring weekly, and there were casualties, both among the escorts and the truckers. In one case the insurgents simply shot the driver of one of the trucks to immobilize it and stop the entire convoy until an Army team could come to the rescue. In another incident involving another one of our teams, they came upon a large Iraqi civilian truck that was stopped in the middle of a narrow road. There was no one around, so the lead escort vehicle followed a dirt track on the side of the road to get around the stationary vehicle. When they got to a certain point along the track, an IED detonated. The IED consisted of explosives attached to a 55-gallon drum of fuel hidden in some brush. The explosives damaged the vehicle and sprayed burning fuel into the open driver's window. Both team members were killed, and their bodies burned along with the vehicle. The nameplates from the doors of their sleeping quarters were added to the names of our other KIAs over the door to the operations center.

This vulnerability meant that we did anything necessary to keep the convoy safe and moving. If other vehicles got too close to the convoy, we would use our up-armored 1-ton pickup trucks to crowd them away. I never rammed another vehicle, and I don't recall hearing anything about anyone on another team doing so, at least not deliberately, but we did anything else we needed to, like giving them a bump from behind to move them along. I got very good at coming close enough to a car that was ignoring our signals to stay away from the convoy to take the side mirror off without causing an accident. I figured that was better than having one of our Kurds get antsy and take a shot at them.

In one incident, a convoy I was escorting was stalled for a considerable length of time in an urban area. We were sitting under a large overpass with buildings on both sides of the road. The trucks were pulled up very close to each other with our gun trucks interspersed along the convoy. It was a high-risk situation, and we had been there long enough that we felt it was prudent to dismount from the vehicles. An Iraqi man in civilian clothes started approaching the convoy across a vacant lot on the side of the road.

Our Kurdish shooters yelled at him in Arabic to stay back and not to come any closer. We could see that he had a large bundle in his arms. We had no idea what he was carrying, but we were not about to let him cross the road and walk between the stationary vehicles. For all we knew he had a bomb that he would either drop as he passed between the trucks and then detonate, or just detonate it in his arms as he got to the right spot and martyr himself. He refused to stop and was arguing with the Kurds who continued yelling at him as he walked toward us.

When he was around 50 meters from the convoy it became apparent that he wasn't going to stop. I reacted by shouldering my M4 and putting the sight on his chest with my finger on the trigger. He stopped with a shocked look on his face and turned around. I realized at that moment that I would have pulled the trigger if he had continued walking. I'm very glad I didn't have to.

The reality was that he was probably just some average guy bringing dinner home to his family, but we had no way of knowing that, and the possibility of a bomb going off between the trucks was a risk we just couldn't take. After the incident was over, the Kurds smiled at me and nodded their support. They knew the score as well as I did. There is no way the average American sitting in their living room can understand the level of risk we were facing on a daily basis and the stress that came with it. Still, the incident emphasized the need to think clearly and keep a level head, rather than just pulling the trigger.

CHAPTER 31

Escalation of Force

Things were so chaotic and dangerous out on the roads and really, anywhere outside the wire, that the military had a set policy for escalation of force (EOF) in the Rules of Engagement (ROE) that specified when lethal force could be used. Because we were armed DoD contractors, we were considered combatants, and expected to adhere to the official EOF procedures followed by all Coalition forces. We were happy to do this. Contrary to how some of the media portrayed security contractors in Iraq, no one wanted to cause the death or injury of an innocent civilian.

The reality was that many Iraqis were relatively clueless when it came to avoiding dangerous and potentially deadly situations. One would think that military vehicles and security contractor trucks and SUVs filled with armed men would be fairly obvious as something to avoid. To further enhance the warnings, many of the contractor vehicles in Iraq carried large white signs on the back that clearly stated in both English and Arabic, "Stay back 100 meters or you will be shot."

That seems like a pretty obvious warning, but many Iraqis coming up on the rear of a PSD team or convey either didn't see it or ignored it. Of course, vehicles approaching a convoy from the side couldn't see a sign on the back of an escort vehicle and may not have recognized what the convoy was. As I said earlier, things on the roads in Iraq were chaotic at the best of times.

So, to prevent collateral damage, a euphemism for civilians being killed or injured, EOF procedures had been established for anyone considered Coalition forces to follow, and that included armed contractors. The EOF consisted of steps to be taken starting with non-lethal signals before any deadly force could be employed. In our case, the tail gunner in every vehicle had the equipment to employ the following steps in this order: a 1,000,000-candlepower handheld spotlight; hand-fired signal flares; hand and arm signals—basically waving their arms and shouting; firing a warning shot into the road off to the side of the approaching vehicle; shooting to disable the vehicle (grille and engine); deadly force against the driver.

Everybody on all the teams knew what the rules were, and the vehicle commanders made sure their Kurdish Peshmerga team members followed them. Like I said, nobody wanted to harm an innocent civilian. But nobody wanted to die or see their teammates die either. There was a procedure, and we followed it even though it potentially reduced our reaction time to a clear threat. Taking the time to employ various non-lethal signals and warnings allowed a vehicle that was a genuine threat to get closer before any decisive action could be taken.

Nevertheless, very few people outwardly complained about following the EOF process. We were there to save lives, not take them. The idea of potentially shooting up a car, and then finding out it had an Iraqi family in it, gave everyone the shivers. The fog of war isn't an excuse for indiscriminate and irresponsible actions. It was too bad the insurgents and their Al Qaida sponsors didn't feel the same way, since their indiscriminate attacks caused hundreds, if not thousands of Iraqi civilian deaths over the years.

CHAPTER 32

Big Bada' Boom!

Limited access entry ramps on expressways are designed so that cars entering the highway can get up to the speed of the passing traffic before entering the traffic flow. The limited access prevents people from pulling onto the highway at zero mph and causing a traffic jam or an accident. They work the same way in Iraq as they do in America. That acceleration lane was a key factor in an event that happened to one of our other teams in the fall of 2004.

The team was escorting a convoy on the main route traveling west out of Baghdad when a car merged off an entrance ramp and onto the expressway at a high rate of speed. It was still accelerating and quickly catching up to the relatively slow-moving convoy. The tail gunner in the last escort truck started going through the EOF procedures by shining a bright spotlight at the car and then shooting a signal flare into the road in front of it. The car showed no signs of slowing down and was getting closer.

The gunner could see that there was a single Iraqi driving the car. He and the other guy in the back of the escort truck both started waving their arms to tell the car to back off. When it didn't, the gunner shot a couple of warning rounds from his PKM machine gun into the road. He later told us the driver of the car seemed to hunch his shoulders down, but the car kept coming. That was a bad sign. The guy obviously knew he was about to be shot at for real and was determined to keep coming.

At that point, the gunner had only seconds to act before the car caught up to the truck he was in, so he took aim and began shooting into the front of the car. The car suddenly exploded with enough force to send a shockwave across the rear of the escort truck. The guys in the other escort vehicles heard and felt the explosion.

The convoy kept moving, so it was impossible to see the effect of the explosion or to investigate what had happened. You don't stop when you're being attacked, if at all possible; you get the trucks you are protecting out of the area. It is highly unlikely that the machine gun rounds detonated whatever was in the car. It's far more likely that the driver either knew he wasn't going to get any closer and detonated the bomb or that he had a dead man switch rigged and was hit by the machine-gun bullets, causing the switch to activate and detonate the explosives. Either way, it was clearly a VBIED and a close call for the team, and it would have been catastrophic had the Kurdish gunner not made the difficult decision to open fire after following the EOF procedure. The incident was reported to the Coalition military, but if they ever uncovered any more information on it, we never heard about it.

That incident had a profound effect on the rest of us since it was proof that we were being targeted by the insurgents. After something like that happens, even if it happens to another team, you begin to view every approaching vehicle as a potential threat. Car bombs are hideously powerful. We had seen the aftermath of them numerous times. The explosions are violent enough to leave a crater in a road or destroy nearby structures. The actual VBIED vehicle is reduced to a few pieces of ragged scrap, and surrounding vehicles are smashed and burned. Human bodies are torn apart and there are frequently puddles of blood on nearby surfaces. We knew and accepted the risks, but that didn't mean we wouldn't do everything we could to mitigate them.

CHAPTER 33

Bullets Hitting a Car Really Do Make Sparks

About a month after the exploding car incident, I was running trail for a convoy, meaning we were the last vehicle. The last escort position in a convoy is critical and busy because you must deal with traffic coming up behind you. It was my regular spot, and my Kurdish crew and I had a lot of experience doing it. Since I was both the vehicle commander and the driver, I had to multitask and split my attention between driving, watching the left side of the roadway, keeping track of what the rest of my crew was doing, and checking the mirrors to see what was going on behind us. Having been a tank platoon leader in the Army, multitasking was something I was used to doing on a regular basis. As usual, we were in a 1-ton up-armored pickup truck with a crew cab and a machine gun in the bed facing back.

There was a doorway cut through the back of the cab so you could move between the cab and the truck bed. I noticed a car gaining on us from behind in the mirror and heard the tail gunner yelling. The shooter who rode in the back seat of the cab got up and went back to join the gunner in the armored bed of the truck. I kept one eye on the mirror to see what was happening. By now both the gunner and the other shooter who had joined him were yelling and waving their arms. The gunner shot a flare into the road and then fired a warning shot to warn the approaching car off, but it didn't slow down. It just kept getting closer.

By now, it was close enough that even looking in the mirror, I could tell at least three military-age males were in the car. The gunner had gone through the EOF procedures by shining the spotlight, shooting a flare, and finally firing a warning shot. There was a big sign on the back of the truck warning cars to stay back 100 meters or they would be shot, but the car was within a few car lengths now. The exploding car the other team encountered only a month earlier was fresh on our minds, and the gunner finally decided he had no choice but to take more extreme action.

I watched in the mirror as he opened fire, aiming for the grille to disable the car. The PKM was mounted on a pintle mount bolted into the bed of the truck and both the car and our truck were still moving down the road, so precise aim wasn't easy. It's weird, the things that pop into your head at any given moment. I watched as the .30 caliber bullets impacted the grille and then up higher on the roof posts and windshield. I recall thinking to myself that bullets really do make sparks when they hit a car, just like in the movies. The car went into a spin and went off the side of the road and out of my range of vision in the mirror.

I reported the incident to the team leader by radio and provided a detailed statement when we got back to camp. The company reported it to the military, and that was the end of it. The fact that there were at least three guys in the car probably means it wasn't a VBIED. But several of us, myself included, had been shot at by insurgents in cars in the past and would be in the future. The warnings and the big sign on the back of the truck should have made it clear to any rational person to stay back, but who can say what was going through their minds? The clear danger was that they were determined to close with us no matter what warnings they got. The bottom line was that we did everything according to the proper Escalation of Force procedure and lived to see another day. It probably sounds strange to say it, but I sincerely hope they were bad guys out to kill us and not just some clueless civilians.

CHAPTER 34

Convoy Escort from Abu Ghraib

The warehouse we worked out of in Abu Ghraib was well known to the insurgents. There's no way they could not have known about it. It was a huge compound right off the main road between Baghdad and Fallujah, and the near-constant traffic of trucks and convoys coming and going made it obvious. Anyone could see that it was something important since it was fortified with a high wall, and a main gate flanked by towers with Russian-made 12.7mm machine guns in them.

To make it difficult for a suicide bomber to ram the gate, the road into the place was blocked with barriers that made it impossible to pull directly into the gate. That meant that convoys trying to enter the compound had to go past the gate, then make a 180-degree turn off the pavement and backtrack up a narrow dirt driveway almost the entire length of the wall before trucks could make the almost 90-degree left turn to negotiate the gate. It made getting into the compound very slow and left you sitting at a dead stop for long periods fronting the busy road. It was easily observable, so the insurgents would have no trouble tracking a convoy to a good ambush location.

The mujahideen tried their best to damage the place. One day, insurgents in a van decided to conduct a drive-by attack on the site. They obviously hadn't thought things through, because as they slowed down and started shooting at the guards in the towers, both towers returned fire with their big 12.7mm machine guns. If you're not familiar with the Russian 12.7 machine gun, it is similar to the American M2 .50 caliber machine gun, at least in terms of power. The towers were manned by Iraqis, although I don't know if they were FPS troops (Facilities Protection Services, an Iraqi paramilitary force) or contract guards. We didn't really care since it wasn't our problem, and the Marines who ran the warehouse complex trusted them. Whoever they were, they knew how to shoot their heavy machine guns. The big bullets will easily punch through light armor or an engine block, and they went through the sides of the van like nothing was there, going in one side and out the other. The shooting stopped abruptly as the van veered off the side of the road and came to a stop on the rough ground.

We didn't see the actual exchange of gunfire, since it happened outside the high walls; all we saw was the aftermath. The van was pretty torn up, and it was obvious whoever was inside wouldn't be in very good condition. Unfortunately for anyone who might have been still alive after the initial exchange of gunfire, no one dared go close to the van to check since everyone was concerned that it might have been a VBIED full of explosives intended to blow the gate. It was a familiar pattern. The insurgents suppress the guards by shooting at them, and then the vehicle full of explosives rams the gate and explodes.

The disabled van, and its no-doubt grisly cargo, sat there for a day before an Army EOD (Explosive Ordnance Disposal) team found time to come to check it out. We never found out what they discovered in the van; it was just gone one day. The Marines at the warehouse said the Army came, and then an Iraqi truck took it away. Even if anyone inside had survived the heavy slugs, which is unlikely, it's doubtful they lasted long bleeding in the back of the van. Just another aspect of a very nasty war.

CHAPTER 35

The Nisour Square Massacre

Things changed considerably for private security contractors in Iraq as a result of the so-called Nisour Square massacre that occurred on September 16, 2007. At least that's what the media started calling it soon after it happened. No one who wasn't there will ever know exactly what happened, or why the guys on the Blackwater team opened fire in the crowded square. Some of them say they were taking fire, and others say they weren't. Although I had acquaintances working for Blackwater, my experience with them was limited. Even though I was accepted for their pre-deployment training program in 2004, I decided to go a different route to get a contract. I do know from personal experience that they would point their guns at SUVs that clearly contained other Western contractors, even when driving inside the Green Zone. That didn't give them a very good reputation among the rest of us, but the guys I knew personally who worked for them were both experienced and level-headed.

As for the Nisour Square incident, all I can say for sure is that it changed private security work in Iraq, but I was out by then, so it didn't affect me personally. The fallout included greater restrictions on private security companies by both the United States and the new Iraqi government. Contractors had to have a license issued by the Iraqi government, and they had to put signs on their vehicles stating their company names so it would be easier to identify them and hold them accountable for their behavior. But perhaps the most far-reaching outcome was the fact that after that incident, private security contractors could formally be held liable and charged for crimes in the United States as a result of their actions in Iraq.

It's easy to judge people and events after the fact, especially if you weren't there when they happened. While witness statements and recreations of events can go a long way to explain the events and what led up to them, the one thing they can never do is reconstruct the stress and fear of being under attack. Something the State Department learned the hard way.

Blackwater had the contract to provide PSD security for employees of the US State Department in Iraq. After the Nisour Square incident, the State Department made a new rule that an officer from the Diplomatic Security Service (DSS) had to accompany all Blackwater-protected movements of State Department personnel in Iraq. In 2010, I was in Baghdad again on a short-term assignment from my then-current employer, a US government contractor who was about to start their first contract in Iraq. As part of that assignment, I went to the US Embassy for a meeting with one of the Assistant Regional Security Officers (ARSO) to talk about the current security situation and get his thoughts on what would be needed to operate safely there. During the conversation over coffee at the embassy DFAC, the topic of the Nisour Square incident and subsequent new rules came up, including the accompaniment of missions by DSS officers.

The ARSO related that the DSS officers had very much changed their tune on PSD teams after accompanying the Blackwater teams on multiple missions. They quickly realized that sitting in a safe room at the embassy telling teams how they should operate and actually being in the vehicles on the roads surrounded by potential threats were two very different things. The DSS officers who were supposed to be overseeing the Blackwater teams quickly gained an appreciation for the chaos of being out on the road and the need to make split-second decisions that could have life-and-death consequences. What happened at Nisour Square was history by then, and the policies in place were not going to change, but it gave me a sense of satisfaction to see that the armchair quarterbacks were finding out the hard way that it wasn't as easy as it looked to provide security in an insurgent conflict zone.

Author on a mission on the road to Mosul. Iraq could be cold in the winter, especially in the northern parts. We had a HUMVEE escort for this part of the trip.

AK rifles bought off the street were well-used and required a lot of TLC to keep them running. Don't let anyone tell you that AKs don't need regular maintenance.

The entrance to the Chinese restaurant is marked by the paper lantern on the right. It wasn't exactly a high-class neighborhood, but the food didn't make us sick and it was better than MREs.

The Suburban we crashed at 75mph on the road to Bayji. The guardrails kept us from taking a long dive into the desert.

My PSD team of Americans and Nepalis on the range at K2. Yam is in the front to my right.

Vehicles got shot up regularly. This one limped back to base on the rim. Note that the rear window is shot out but the bulletproof glass behind it is intact.

An up-armored Suburban hit by a roadside EFP bomb. The molten copper went through the armor plate like it wasn't even there, instantly killing the two men in the back seat.

Saddam built the Flintstones-style house for his grandchildren. It included a kitchen and elevator and must have been a lot of fun for the kids lucky enough to play there while many others lived in poverty.

A stationary convoy was a sitting target. One of the Pesh keeps a watchful eye on things.

The author in front of one of the massive busts of Saddam that used to rest atop the Republican Palace. Saddam's ego was as big as the statue.

The author inside one of the giant replicas of Saddam's hands that hold the arched swords up in Baghdad.

The crossed swords are a familiar landmark in Baghdad.

The souk was interesting and fun the day I went. Three days after this picture was taken, it was bombed by insurgents, killing and wounding both contractors and locals, and closed, never to reopen.

Traffic in Iraq had a few differences from life back in the States. An armored Excursion and an M1 tank pass on the road.

The author with his Peshmerga vehicle crew on the convoy escort contract. The guy to my right is the one who almost shot me with a machine gun.

Insurgent attacks weren't the only hazard on the road. The infrastructure was in bad condition after the invasion.

Attempts to make Christmas more cheerful usually had the opposite effect, but you can give the artist a capital "E" for effort.

The "trunk monkey" serves as a tail gunner for the last vehicle in a convoy. This one is armed with a Russian PKM 7.62mm machine gun.

B6 Excursions were tough. This one was hit with a VBIED just before I came on board the contract. The explosion left the vehicle on its roof, but everyone escaped with only minor injuries.

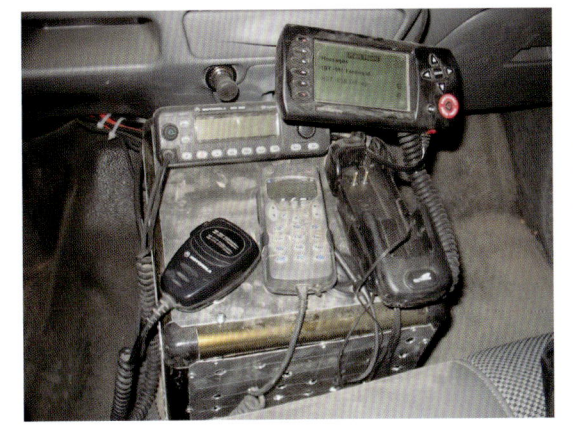

All the vehicles had radios, GPS, and trackers that indicated the vehicle's position on screens in the operation room. The red button is the "panic button" that notified the ops room the vehicle had been hit.

Detours to avoid suspicious checkpoints on the road could be long and difficult, but they were better than getting attacked or abducted by insurgents posing as Iraqi troops.

A Stryker links up with our convoy on the road. Sometimes we had Army escorts if the area was exceptionally dangerous, and we were escorting highly sensitive cargo.

The author on the range at the Baghdad Police Academy. The place was bombed regularly by insurgents, but it was a nice range, so we went anyway.

The author shakes hands with the commanding general of the Iraqi 13th Infantry Division. He provided a nice lunch, but I avoided the fish caught in the sewage-polluted Euphrates River.

Handing out humanitarian supplies to the people living in the ruins of the abandoned theater quickly turned into a free-for-all.

Gurkhas

Nepalis make great soldiers, as witnessed by the British Army having at least one Gurkha unit active from 1815 to the present day. They are tough, loyal, and tenacious. I worked with Nepalese men on a couple of my contracts. Some were actual former British Gurkhas while others were former members of the Nepali Army. Other than the fact that in some cases the two groups had different terms in their contracts, there was no real way for us on the teams to tell the difference at a glance.

As far as we were concerned, they were all just Gurkhas. They were friendly and most spoke good enough English to sit and shoot the breeze with. They liked football (soccer to Americans) and cricket, so as long as we could converse intelligently on either, we could talk sports. But in general, they kept to themselves most of the time when they were off duty. They definitely had a different outlook on personal space. At one point I and another American were living on one side of a trailer at Camp Laramore-Matthews just off the main north–south route through Bayji. Two of the Gurkhas lived in the room at the other end of the trailer, and we shared the bathroom. It wasn't unusual to go into the bathroom and find a dozen pairs of colorful underwear hung up to dry everywhere. When they could find the right ingredients, they even prepared some of their own food. They had their own culture, and they were smart and utterly reliable as team members.

CHAPTER 36

Conflict Resolution—Gurkha Style

Gurkhas liked to drink. A lot. When we were posted to the company area outside of Radwaniyah in Baghdad, the Gurkhas had their own building and were assigned a Suburban to use for laundry, chow, and PX runs. It just seemed simpler that way than to have them try to schedule one of the vehicles the rest of us used for admin runs. Regardless of General Order Number 1 and the prohibition of alcohol for anyone under DoD authority (as we were), we always had a lot of booze available. Beer mostly, but some hard stuff too. Alcohol, combined with the fact that the Nepali warrior class consists of exceptionally tough people who may not have had the best social skills, made for some volatile moments.

It was an off day, with no PSD missions scheduled, so other than the stand-by team, everyone was lounging around. Our camp consisted of several Iraqi vacation houses running along canals just outside the Radwaniyah compound where Saddam's buddies used to hang out. The Gurkhas had all been drinking since around lunchtime, so they were pretty well-oiled by midafternoon. Apparently, there was a minor scheduling dispute as to who was going to use their Suburban to either make a PX run or to take clothes to the laundry. I have no idea why it wasn't possible to do both, but to them it wasn't.

You have to understand that these were some seriously tough guys. Peaceful discourse and mild discussion weren't really a part of their culture. Just ask the Japanese troops they fought in World War II. They also loved their knives. Very few had actual kukri knives like you see in the movies, but they all carried a big nasty knife of some flavor or other. As the discussion became more and more heated, the knives began to come out.

They'd had several other disputes over various things, and the team leaders had warned them to keep things under control. Fortunately, one of the cooler heads, and probably tougher Gurkhas, had intervened before anyone got cut.

Unfortunately, the loser of the argument wasn't satisfied with the outcome. He figured if he couldn't use the Suburban that day, no one else was going to use it either. His solution was to take his large knife and stab each of the tires until the Suburban was sitting there on the rims. Consequently, no one went to the PX or dropped their laundry off that day, and they had to find another way to the DFAC for chow.

What they did get was the use of another Suburban to go and buy four new tires, get them mounted on the rims to the Suburban, and then put new tires on it. As far as I know, no one ever got in any trouble over the incident. In the greater scheme of things, it just didn't matter all that much.

CHAPTER 37

"Oh, no, Sir. I'm fine"

When I first started working PSD in Iraq in 2004, the insurgents weren't quite as sophisticated as they'd become by 2006. We were making many of our runs in soft-skin Suburban SUVs. The clients rode in B6-level armored Ford Excursions, but we rode in soft-skinned vehicles. Anyone who has ever shot even a handgun into a vehicle body knows that even a 9mm bullet will go right through it and probably come out on the other side.

In the fall of 2004, most insurgent attacks were with small arms, either from the side of the road or from another vehicle. One such attack occurred on Route 1 while the team it happened to was returning to Baghdad from Fallujah. As they passed through an area where there were a few scraggly trees, several Iraqis started shooting at the three-vehicle convoy. The guys in the lead and trailing vehicles returned fire and the team kept moving as per standard PSD procedures. There were a couple of holes in the bodywork and the rear side window was shot out of one Suburban, but nothing serious enough to even delay the team.

The team leader got a quick status, and everyone reported that they were fine. The mission continued and the team returned to our camp at the end of the day. Everyone at camp gathered to look at the bullet holes and broken glass in the Suburban and to get the story from the team. Nothing significant, just another day in Iraq. But when Sang, one of the Gurkhas, climbed out of the Suburban, someone noticed that he had blood on his dark T-shirt. Sang was the trunk monkey, the guy who rode in the very back of the trail Suburban, and no one had gotten a close look at him since the attack.

Upon closer examination, it was discovered that a bullet had passed through his left shoulder just above his body armor. It had gone through and hadn't shattered any bones, so his arm, while stiff, was still mobile. As our medic, a former special forces guy, got Sang's armor and shirt off and checked him out, Sang kept repeating that he was fine. Of course, leadership wasn't having any of that, and they had the medic run him to the Army medical facility to get checked out and treated.

The AK round that hit Sang was a standard military full metal jacket (FMJ) bullet that didn't expand or fragment, so it wasn't a terribly serious wound. It had passed straight through his shoulder without hitting anything vital and he was back in camp in a few hours. Leadership said they would be sending him home to recover, but Sang was arguing about the decision. He was worried that, since there was a prohibition on Nepalis working in Iraq, if he went home to Nepal to recover, the government there might not let him return to work in Iraq. The money for PSD work was very good when compared to what he could earn working a job in Nepal, and he didn't want to take a chance of losing the income. In the end, he was given a ticket to Singapore and left on the payroll so he could stay there and recover before coming back. That wasn't destined to work out, but that's another story.

Sang was typical of the Nepalese I knew. Tough, stoic, and not willing to let anything as minor as a gunshot wound interfere with a job he enjoyed and that paid well.

CHAPTER 38

Literal Is as Literal Does

In the summer of 2006, I had a security position with a DoD contractor whose main camp was located in the Green Zone. It was a fortified camp and had Nepali static guards. Nepalese are dedicated and tenacious, and they are also very literal in interpreting their orders. If you told one of them to stand at a certain place until you returned and then didn't return for 24 hours, he would still be standing exactly where you told him to. No questions, no excuses, he would be there.

Because the Green Zone was considered inside the wire, expats could sign out soft-skin vehicles to drive themselves to meetings, the DFAC, the PX, and wherever else they needed to go. There was no need for a PSD team, as long as they stayed in the Green Zone. All they had to do was sign a vehicle out with the guards. Most were smaller SUVs and sedans, but the company had a few nicer vehicles reserved for their director-level guys. The guards had a list with the names of the people eligible to use those special vehicles. Being their head of security, I had my own assigned vehicle, so I didn't have to worry about signing one out, which was a nice perk.

The company's regional vice president for the Middle East would come to see how the projects were doing several times a year. He'd been there often enough that he knew his way around the camp and the Green Zone and didn't need a babysitter. One day he wanted to go to lunch on his own and went to sign out a car. The only vehicles still available were the ones reserved for directors, so he asked for one of them.

The guards dutifully checked his name against the list and informed him that since he was not on the list, he couldn't sign out a car. After that, the conversation went something like this:

VP: "You know who I am, right?"
Guard: "Yes, Sir."

VP: "Then you know that everyone on that list works for me. I'm their boss, right?"
Guard: "Yes, Sir."
VP: "I outrank everyone else here in the camp."
Guard: Yes, Sir."
VP: "Then you can let me take one of the cars."
Guard: "No, Sir. Your name is not on the list."

The conversation went on for a few more minutes, but short of physically trying to take one of the cars, the visiting executive realized he was not going to get a car from that guard. He called around until he found one of the other expats who could come and take him to the DFAC for lunch. To his credit, he wasn't upset at the guards. In fact, he thought it was pretty funny and admired the guard for following orders. Something a lot of senior military officers might want to emulate. When you give someone orders, especially in a conflict zone, you don't give him a hard time for carrying them out.

Firepower

When you serve in the military, the government issues you with the gun they want you to carry. Most of the time in the US, that's some flavor of M16/M4 carbine. For a few, it might be a SAW or a machine gun. Sidearms have run the spread from the old Colt 1911 up through the Sigs being issued today. During the Iraq War, the troops who carried sidearms were issued the Beretta M9 pistol.

That's not the case when you're a contractor. When you're a private security contractor, you generally carry whatever your employer issues you unless you can find something better on your own. I carried quite a few different kinds of guns while I was in Iraq, and I saw other contractors carry some I didn't. They weren't always ideal, and sometimes they were a lot less than that, but they were what we had so we made the most of them.

Most international security companies have an armorer whose job is to maintain the company's weapons and see that they are issued to the contractors doing the work. Sometimes these armorers just stick with whatever the company provides, and other times they go out on the economy and "procure" additional weapons that they think might be useful.

This has resulted in some interesting weapons showing up without an explanation. I've seen everything from grenade launchers to RPGs finding their way into security company arms rooms. Once, I ran across some old Chinese-manufactured frag grenades that have such a bad reputation for erratic fuse settings that I would be surprised if anyone had the nerve to try one out let alone carry one on a mission. Other more common firearms included 1911 and CZ75 pistols. Of course, with non-standard items, the next challenge is finding accessories like magazines.

At other times, items that were considered mission essential were in ridiculously short supply. On one contract where we were issued Glock 17 pistols, we only had one magazine per person. I eventually had someone back in the States buy some and mail them to me. We were also short on 9mm ammunition, which really seems surprising. Fortunately, I was able to source some from some guys I knew and loaded my roommate and myself up.

CHAPTER 39

Arming on the Cheap

Back in the Wild West days of Iraq, just after the invasion in 2003 and up through at least 2006, the quickest and cheapest way to arm a private security force was to literally hand someone a duffle bag full of cash and send them out to buy some guns and ammo on the street. What novels and movies like to call the black market. Most of the guns procured this way had been "liberated" from the Iraqi military and generally had a lot of miles on them. Don't believe it when someone tells you an AK will run forever. They are, for the most part, durable and reliable, but I saw more than a few AKs that were nothing more than an odd-shaped club.

Guns bought on the street included AKs, HK G3s, MP5s, FNs, and Browning Hi-Power pistols. I even knew one guy who found a World War II British Sterling 9mm submachine gun someplace and carried it in the vehicle when we were doing PSD runs. Definitely a novelty gun since we had access to MP5s when we needed a submachine gun, but as the South Africans say, he was chuffed to have it.

Of course, arming on the cheap has its predictable drawbacks. For starters, everything you buy on the street, even in Iraq, has probably been stolen from somewhere: Iraqi government armories and warehouses, weapons shipments, and military unit arms rooms. That didn't really matter in the early days in Iraq since the country was awash in AKs and Browning Hi-Power pistols, and the government that was supposed to be accountable for them didn't exist anymore. However, at one point I gained possession of an M4 that had "Property of U.S. Government" stamped on the receiver. It wasn't anything special so I saw no advantage in taking the risk of keeping it, so I turned it over to the Army to deal with.

Another drawback to arming on the cheap is that you end up with a lot of junk mixed in with the serviceable weapons. More than once I had to go through several AKs to find one that was reliable enough for me to carry it on missions. Not something you want to discover when someone is shooting at you, and you are trying to shoot back.

CHAPTER 40

AKs for Days

By far the most common rifle used by private security contractors was the AKM, also called the AK47 although that wasn't completely accurate since the AKM was a later model. Every Westerner working as a security contractor was issued an AK at some time or another. They were easy to obtain, and ammunition was plentiful. They were designed to be used by uneducated Russian peasants way back in 1947, hence the name AK47, and they were simple enough that even people who had never shot one before could learn to use them quickly. They are also cheap to manufacture and multiple countries besides Russia have manufactured them. There have probably been almost 200 million AK-style guns built and they are used by government forces, insurgents, and terrorists all over the world.

Many of the ones bought off the street in Iraq were in rough condition. Some were genuine Russian manufacture sent to Saddam back in the days of the Soviet Union, while others came from just about every country that ever built one. Since there was no system to account for them, if one of the street purchases didn't work the security company arms room guy would just toss it in the canal and that was the end of it. They were adequate, and the 7.62×39 cartridge was pretty good and had decent penetration against cars.

Static guards were usually issued the full wooden stock version, but we were issued the version with an under-folding metal stock. This was because we spent a lot of time in vehicles and had to be able to maneuver the gun and return fire from inside a moving vehicle. In that situation, a folding stock is an advantage even though it is difficult to shoot accurately with the stock folded up.

I was never a big fan of the AK. The ergonomics suck and it has a lot of rough edges. Changing the magazine is also slower than with an M4/AR because of the way the AK magazine tilts in and out rather than just dropping the empty magazine straight down and pushing a full one straight up to reload. I know a lot of people in the US are fans and claim the AK is better than the M4, but I've used both on a daily basis and like the M4 much better. But the AKs worked well enough. Some of the guys either really liked them or knew they weren't going to get anything else and spent money out of their own pockets to customize them to make them more ergonomic and effective. Like them or not, they were the most common firearm in use by contractors in Iraq.

CHAPTER 41

Submachine Guns

You might think the next most common firearm issued to contractors was the M4, and I suppose that might be the case. But in my experience, it was the Heckler and Koch MP5 submachine gun. Every team of contractors had them whether their primary weapons were AKs or M4s. They weren't much use at longer ranges or against a vehicle since they were chambered for the standard 9mm Luger pistol cartridge, but they were excellent for close-quarters or low-profile assignments. We used them for close protection in buildings when I was doing PSD work. They are compact, easy to maneuver, and far less obtrusive than an M4 or AK.

We had some that were suppressed, again bought on the black market. It would be interesting to know how many Iraqi armories were cleaned out by Iraqi troops when they knew they were going to lose and bailed on the Army. It had to be a lot because there were plenty of ex-Iraqi military guns on the market.

The cities and villages were full of packs of feral dogs during the war. They may still be, since most Iraqis, and Muslims in general, don't like dogs or keep them as pets. They see them as unclean animals. The dogs were hungry and vicious, and rabies wasn't uncommon. Sometimes guys would take the suppressed MP5s out at night to reduce the feral dog population. Being suppressed doesn't make a gun silent like in the movies, but they were a lot quieter than an unsuppressed M4. We didn't want to cause a general alarm by shooting at night.

Doing night patrols when I was at the pump station project was particularly exciting at times, because of packs of vicious dogs. The construction site was huge and there were few exterior lights on at night since there wasn't any work going on after dark. There was also a danger of being shot at from across the Euphrates River at night and lights would have made it easier to hit the security guys in the towers or walking the perimeter. Walking around with your flashlight on all the time was also not a great idea, so we relied on our familiarity with the terrain and acclimating our eyes to the darkness to know where we were and find our way, only using our flashlights if we heard or saw something unusual. That meant that you were usually alerted to the presence of dogs by the sounds of snarling and growling. We were hesitant to shoot at them, even with suppressed guns, because we couldn't be sure bullets fired in the dark wouldn't go somewhere you didn't want them to, and we didn't want to shoot someone or something important by mistake. That frequently left us with only yelling and throwing rocks to drive the dogs off long enough for us to back off and get clear of them. There were also jackals running around, a wild animal that looked like a smaller version of a coyote, but they usually avoided humans.

The MP5 wasn't a gun I would want to take into a full-blown firefight against enemies shooting AKs or for trying to stop an oncoming vehicle, but for close-in or low-profile work, they were great. They also had a definite "coolness" factor to them, even though the 9mm cartridge was relatively weak compared to a rifle cartridge.

CHAPTER 42

America's Rifle

Regardless of what many armchair gun experts say, I'm a fan of the M4. You can go to gun forums and still see comments from people who don't like the M16 because they were unreliable when they were first issued to our troops in Vietnam in 1964. But that was a long time ago, and they have been modified and perfected since then. They're ergonomic, accurate, and easy to take care of and I was pleased to be issued one on a couple of different contracts. The first was a semiautomatic Bushmaster SBR (Short Barreled Rifle) when I was doing convoy escort work. The short 14-inch barrel made it more manageable in a vehicle.

As I've explained elsewhere, we had Kurds working with us as shooters. They carried AKs and RPK squad automatic weapons, both of which shot the same 7.62×39 cartridge. They were the epitome of spray and pray, and usually shot on full auto. They may not have been the best shots, but at least they put out a good volume of fire to keep the other guy's head down.

Since all the vehicle drivers were Americans, putting out a high volume of fire wasn't our job; driving and commanding the vehicle was. But we were also better shots than the Kurds, so the company had a standing order that if there was an enemy that the Kurds couldn't hit, they were supposed to get one of the Americans. When you're placing your shots, semi-auto is just what you need.

The second M4 I had was a beautiful brand-new Colt selective fire M4. It was smooth as butter and a dream to shoot. I had it when I was the site security manager at that remote project site outside of Nasiriya that was surrounded by hostile militias. M4s were great because there was so much gear you could customize them with. The company provided us with EOTech reflex sights, lights, and other goodies we could mount on our personal weapons. Regardless of what some people say about their reliability, I never had a failure in the dusty Iraqi environment. Definitely my favorite firearm of everything I carried over there and one I would never trade for an AK.

CHAPTER 43

Sidearms

All the Western contractors had a handgun along with their rifles. Most often it was a locally procured Browning Hi-Power. These were the original items complete with a magazine disconnect safety and the lousy trigger that goes with it. Hi-Powers were everywhere and very easy to acquire since they had been the official sidearm of the Iraqi Army. Since they shot the same 9mm that everything else did, the ammo was usually plentiful as well. It was a utilitarian gun that got the job done, but it wasn't one of my personal favorites.

The other most common contractor handgun was the Glock 17. It was ultra-reliable, which made it perfect for the harsh desert environment. There was always a layer of dust on everything, inside and outside, and we had plenty of days when the dust in the air was so thick it looked like it was foggy outside. The kind of environment where a Glock really shines. They were also light compared to the Hi-Power, and plenty accurate.

During my last contract, our employer issued us brand new Kimber 1911s. That was unusual since .45 ACP ammunition was a lot harder to source than 9mm, so they sent over 30,000 rounds along with the guns. It was a sweet gun, and other contractors that saw us with them often mentioned they wished they had .45s. Since I still also had a Hi-Power, I'd carry the 1911 in my drop leg holster and leave the Hi-Power in the cross-draw holster on my vest. That way I could drop my vest and gear but still have a gun on me.

Handguns are underpowered compared to rifles, and they aren't much use in a general firefight but they have their place. They are easy to carry around, so you can always be armed if you have one. I literally didn't go anywhere unarmed, including the PX and DFAC. There were just too many variables and I refused to be unarmed where a guerrilla war was being fought. I also slept with my handgun within easy reach of my bed. Maybe some people would see it as a security blanket, but I felt better knowing I could reach out a couple of inches and have it in my hand. There were always Iraqis around in our camps. We hired them for camp maintenance, cleaning, and working on the vehicles. The reality of it was I just didn't trust Iraqis in general and I felt better if I was armed all the time. A handgun made that possible.

But even though they aren't an ideal weapon in a firefight, they are very useful if you are in a vehicle. More than once guys on the teams deployed their handgun from inside a vehicle much more quickly than their teammates were able to get their AK or M4 pointed in the right direction. This was especially useful if the threat was very close or at an odd angle in relation to the vehicle, which made getting a rifle pointed at it difficult.

CHAPTER 44

When You Want Something More

At one point one of the senior guys on one of my contracts (we'll call him Bob) decided we needed something chambered in 7.62 NATO for use in the vehicles to stop an oncoming car and as a designated marksman rifle because it is a larger cartridge and packs a greater punch than either the 5.56 fired by American M4s, or the 7.62×39 the AK47 shoots. After some searching, he found an Army armorer who had a bunch of FNs that had been captured from the Iraqis. They were old-style FN FAL rifles that were probably made back in the 1960s, but they were in good shape. They were just sitting around the guy's arms room, so Bob developed a relationship with the guy and struck up a deal.

General Order Number 1, as applied to troops in Iraq, forbade the possession or consumption of alcohol. Technically, as contractors working on DoD contracts, the order applied to us too, but no one ever enforced it or even checked on us to see if we were complying. That meant that Bob could easily get his hands on plenty of hard alcohol like bourbon and Scotch whisky. Just the thing to trade to the armorer for a couple of dozen obsolete FN rifles.

It seemed like a good deal for a while. The rifles were in decent condition, and they did pack a punch compared to either an M4 or an AK. Then, Army CID (Criminal Investigation Division) got wind of it. By the time the dust settled, I and several of the other security contractors on the contract had to give statements to CID. That was not something any of us wanted to do. Bob was soon gone, sent back to the States with no job, and the rifles had been turned over to the Army. We never did find out what, if anything, happened to the armorer. Probably not much, but who can say? The lesson was simple; keep a low profile. The reality was that Bob could probably have sourced some FNs, or HKs, from locals out in the community and nobody would have cared. Dragging a soldier into the situation by trading him contraband whisky for guns was a bad idea. When is a secret not a secret? As soon as more than one person knows it.

CHAPTER 45

Oddball Stuff

There were lots of oddball weapons around. It was the Middle East after all. I saw old Soviet-era guns like the SKS in the hands of locals. One of our teams had a Dragunov SVD with an old Russian scope they'd picked up somewhere. It worked well and used the same Russian 7.62×51R ammunition as our PKM machine guns, so it made a decent designated marksman rifle.

I mentioned that one of our guys had picked up a Sterling somewhere. The Sterling was designed back in 1944 but was manufactured as recently as 1988, so no clue where it came from, but it could have been bouncing around since World War II. It wasn't as effective as an MP5, but it worked, and he thought it was cool. I had to admit it had a certain romanticism to it.

I acquired an old M1 Garand, but it was in terrible condition. Even if I could have gotten it working, there was no source for clips or ammunition, so it sat in the corner of my hooch for a long time until I moved on to another contract. In general, the place was a gun lover's dream come true. There were all sorts of guns around and virtually no restrictions on carrying or shooting them. I definitely had a lot of fun and shot every kind of gun I could get my hands on.

In one notable case of a team having top-of-the-line gear, I saw a team carrying FN P90s. They had pulled into the parking lot of the Green Zone PX just as I had got out of my vehicle. They caught my eye because they were driving Mercedes SUVs. When they got out, I noticed they were all armed with FN P90s. It's a rather exotic-looking weapon made in Belgium by FN Herstal that shoots an intermediate 5.7×28mm cartridge and was originally designed as a replacement for the MP5. It's an unusual cartridge that is both expensive and much harder to source than the standard military cartridges the rest of us used. I couldn't tell what kind of handguns they were carrying, but I wouldn't be surprised if they were FN Five-seveN pistols, which shoot the same cartridge as the P90. Whoever they were, their employer didn't spare any expense when they equipped them.

Working with Russians

As I write this, the Russian invasion of Ukraine plods on. Russia is in the news a lot, but most Americans have no personal experience with anyone from Russia. Odd as it sounds, my time in Iraq gave me some direct personal experience working with and around Russians.

In general, I found Russians to be gruff and grumpy, as well as very headstrong. I once had a neighbor in the States who had a mail-order bride from Ukraine, and she never had anything good to say about Russians, and that was long before they invaded her homeland. It was an eye-opener working with them, and not without its elements of comic relief.

CHAPTER 46

Don't Travel Through Kuwait

One of the projects I did security for was a massive pump station in southern Iraq. It was a typical Middle Eastern development project funded internationally and worked on in a start-again-stop-again pattern over the years. This one had started back in 1983 but had never been finished. My employer was providing engineers and construction managers, but all the work was being sourced out to local Iraqi and various international contractors. Since the pumps for the project had originally been manufactured and provided by the then-Soviet Union, they imported a couple of dozen Russian engineers to work on them.

The Russians didn't have visas or US-issued Common Access Cards (CAC) and since they were not members of the Coalition, they had no official route to enter the country. To get around this, our employer gave them letters signed by the DoD Contracting Office authorizing them to travel and work in Iraq on the project. The letters were very specific regarding where they could enter the country, so they were told in no uncertain terms that this was a less-than-ideal situation and that they were only to enter Iraq by flying in from Amman, Jordan to Baghdad. Our employer would provide transportation from Baghdad to Nasiriyah and back as necessary. Even though Nasiriyah was in southern Iraq, they were specifically told not to try to travel back and forth to Kuwait because their letters would not allow them back into the country from there if they left.

Inevitably, a group of them ignored their instructions and decided to drive from Nasiriyah to Kuwait for some reason, probably to go shopping or spend a night in a nice hotel since their camp was pretty spartan. Four of them hopped in a car one evening and headed south toward Kuwait. They showed the Iraq border guards their letters as they left Iraq. The border guards didn't care if they wanted to leave Iraq and let them pass. There was around a kilometer of empty road between the Iraqi border station and the Kuwait border.

When the Russians reached the Kuwaiti border, they showed the Kuwaiti guards their letter. Predictably, the Kuwaiti guards didn't recognize a letter from a US contractor authorizing the Russians to enter Iraq as being sufficient to enter Kuwait. The Russians were refused entry and turned around.

When they reached the Iraqi border, the guards there indicated in no uncertain terms that they couldn't care less about the Russians' letter and refused them entry into Iraq. This left the four Russians between a rock and a hard place. They couldn't get into Kuwait, and they couldn't get back into Iraq, so they were stuck in the no-man's-land between the two countries. Their predicament was compounded by a heavy rainstorm that began about that time. Anyone familiar with the desert knows that heavy rains usually mean flooding since the desert soil doesn't absorb water very well.

The Russians, now trapped in a car on a 1-kilometer stretch of highway between the two border stations, began to phone frantically for help. They had no food or water in the car and the rainwater was starting to rise to the edge of the road. Their boss in Baghdad began calling everyone from our employer to us, demanding we rescue their people. I was in Baghdad at the time, as were all the senior people from our employer, and the Russians in question were stuck some 500 kilometers away so there wasn't a lot we could quickly do. Eventually, they were rescued the next day by a security team from one of the projects in southern Iraq, but they had a rough night sitting in their car in the middle of nowhere.

I have no idea what possessed the Russians to ignore the very clear instructions not to go to Kuwait. My subsequent contact with the same group of Russians when I was assigned to the pump station project left me with the impression that they were drunk much of the time, and when they were sober, their attitudes were so bad they wouldn't listen to anything anyone tried to tell them. One would think they might have learned something during the night they spent in a car sitting in the dark awaiting rescue, but apparently not.

CHAPTER 47

Vodka and a Pet Turkey

I was transferred to Nasiriyah in the winter of 2006 to take over responsibility for managing the security of the pump station project. It was a huge 400-acre facility with smaller camps inside the boundaries for the various factions working there. We had a camp for our engineers and construction managers that included a PSD team and Nepalese static guards. The Russians, including the same ones who had gotten themselves trapped on the highway a few months previously, had their own compound within the station boundaries. There were about 20 of them.

Weekends in the Middle East are Friday and Saturday. Friday is the day for going to the mosque, and Saturday is the day off. The Russians would all disappear on Thursday afternoon, and no one would see them outside their camp again until sometime Sunday. I eventually found out that they would begin drinking on Thursday afternoon and wouldn't stop until late Saturday night. They would come back to work on Sunday.

They didn't like Americans and blamed us for the unsafe conditions when working in Iraq. I suppose they were right since it was the United States and not Russia the Iraqis were angry at. One night we took a couple of RPG rockets and some machine-gun fire from across the river. It blew one of the Nepalese guards out of the watch tower facing the river (he survived) and stitched some bullets through a couple of buildings. One of those was one of the Russian living quarters. The line of bullet holes was just above where one of them had been sleeping that night.

I had to go to their camp for something one day. When I got there, I noticed a white domestic turkey wandering around. The kind you see in a barnyard and later eat for Thanksgiving. I guess I was someone new it hadn't seen before, so it trundled up to me and proceeded to follow me around the camp until I went into one of the buildings. It turned out the Russians had the live turkey flown in to cook for Christmas dinner the previous year, but after it was there for a while, they got attached to it and let it wander around their camp.

I was actually more than a little surprised that the Russians could be sentimental enough to get attached to it. Good thing for the turkey, though. When my employer finally pulled out of the project, the Russians stayed on since only they knew much about the pumps at the station. The bird looked pretty rough, and who can blame it considering the climate in the desert, but as far as I knew it was still alive when we eventually left the site. Who can say if they decided to eat it when they finally left? It was pretty scrawny when I saw it and I doubt it got any better with more time in the desert.

Downtime

We weren't always busy when working on security contracts. In fact, there was a lot of downtime since each team usually only did three to four missions a week, although most of those missions lasted all day. Missions were stressful, and it was good to have time to decompress, especially if a team had experienced a couple of high-tempo missions or incidents. Along with that, the number of missions was reliant on the client's needs. If they weren't moving around, or there weren't any convoys on the schedule, we didn't have anything to do other than each team taking a rotation as the on-call team in case the client had a sudden need. Some of our downtime was also taken up with training to keep our skills sharp and develop new tactics to deal with the evolving situation on the ground.

But other than those exceptions, our off time was our own. Since we were working in what the government called a "conflict zone," we couldn't go out on the town to go to a movie or out to dinner. Because we had CAC cards, we could make use of the facilities like recreation centers and gyms put in place for the troops, but they were fairly small and usually weren't located close to our camps. Consequently, we had to find ways to entertain ourselves or risk going stir-crazy from boredom.

CHAPTER 48

Training

Everyone I worked with on the teams was prior military, except for a couple of guys who were former police officers. But even they were former SWAT types who had some strong tactical backgrounds. Nevertheless, there was mandatory training for each team on a regular basis to keep our skills up and make sure that everyone was on the same sheet of music when there was an incident or special mission.

Team training covered different areas. There was quite a bit of mobile training that covered vehicle movement, on both PSD missions and convoy escort. We would find somewhere we could go that had room and didn't have a lot of traffic so we could run drills. Saddam's parade ground under the swords was a good place if we were close enough to use it. For PSD missions, we practiced actions when taking fire, IED response, disabled vehicle drills, and client movement. We would take the whole team out, including the client vehicle, and practice how to cross-load team members or the clients from one vehicle to another if one of the vehicles was disabled. We had several instances where that training was critical when vehicles were disabled for real, like when my team had one of our vehicles totaled in a traffic accident. When our crash occurred, we were able to get everyone, and their gear, loaded into another vehicle and be on our way just six minutes after the collision occurred.

We also did training in close protection (CP) techniques when the clients were on foot. Learning how to move in a formation with the clients in the center, while keeping a good lookout in all directions, takes practice. We practiced standard CP formations like the box formation and the diamond formation and ensured everyone knew their duties as the point man, flank guards, or rear guard. It sounds easy if you're just moving across an open area, but it gets a lot more complicated when the terrain is rough or broken up by vegetation or man-made objects and buildings.

Individual training was the most enjoyable. Driving training covered skills like backing up at high speed, doing J-turns, crossing curbs without blowing out your tires, blocking out another vehicle, and running roadblocks. As you can imagine, it was a lot of fun practicing the maneuvers at high speeds. Again, Saddam's parade ground was an excellent place to practice.

We spent quite a bit of time on the range. We had to stay sharp on moving and shooting with both our rifles and handguns. We also had to practice staying in the fight if we were wounded. For example, if you were right-handed and your right arm was injured, you had to be able to switch to left-handed shooting and still be effective. We also did familiarity training with different weapons. We had a variety of firearms to shoot, everything from AKs to FNs to HKs, and we learned to be proficient with them all. Of course, after shooting we got to have the fun of cleaning all the guns. To be honest, I've never minded cleaning guns, it's almost like a Zen exercise to me. You just zone out and lose track of everything except disassembling the gun, cleaning it, and then putting it back together.

Finally, there was medical training. We had several guys who were former special forces medics, and they really knew their stuff. They trained or refreshed us in all the usual tasks like assessing the wound or injury, stopping the bleeding, dressing wounds, CPR, and splinting to immobilize a fracture. We also had to learn how to administer an IV. That could be critical if a team member or client had lost a lot of blood and it would be a while before they could be medevaced out for treatment, especially in a climate like Iraq. We learned by practicing on each other, no practice dummies for us. We would insert the needle into the other guy and hook him up to a bag of saline. Aside from being good practice, the saline was good for the recipient since everyone was on the edge of being dehydrated half the time anyway by wearing armor and gear in 100+ degree heat. You had to be careful not to collapse a vein or create a hematoma. Most of the guys were pretty good at it, but there was one guy I made sure I never partnered up with.

The training was fun, and everyone took it seriously. We all knew we might have to use any of the skills we learned and practiced for real on the next mission we ran.

CHAPTER 49

Killing Time

When we weren't on a mission, standby, or training, our time was our own. There were plenty of vehicles to use, and everybody had a phone in case they were needed, so you didn't have to hang around camp. We had Common Access Cards, so we could use the small recreation centers set up on some of the larger bases. They were either run by the military or the USO, and had pool tables and foosball tables, along with a few other things. Some also had video games, but the military had a strict regulation forbidding any games set in the Middle East so they wouldn't offend the locals. That meant that games like *Conflict: Desert Storm* were out. We wondered how a game like that could offend the locals since they weren't allowed in the rec centers anyway, but whatever. *HALO* was always popular. There were also gyms on the bases, so you could run on a treadmill or lift weights.

There were a few places where you could go to a pool. The mansion my first employer had in the Mansour district of Baghdad had a really nice pool we used when we were there. There was also a pool in the Green Zone that was okay. They used to have swimsuit contests that some of the female soldiers entered. They could never leave their M4 anywhere, so it was funny to see them walk by in their bikini carrying their rifle. When I was assigned up at K2, the guys built a pool by bulldozing out a hole in the ground and lining it with an ultra-heavy-duty tarp. Then they put HESCOS around it and covered it with a camouflage net for a little shade. It wasn't very big, but at least you could jump in and get cooled off. We had to change the water every few days though, or it would get gross.

There weren't very many places to go out and eat, which was why the Chinese place in the Green Zone was nice. Unfortunately, even if you could find a local place on the edge of a base that was safe to go to, the Iraq version of kitchen hygiene wasn't quite the same as the American version. I ended up getting food poisoning twice, which finally cured me of wanting to eat locally prepared food. There were also little stands by the roads where locals would set up rusty grills and roast whole chickens to sell. Pete, one of the guys I worked with, loved those things and was always stopping to get one. Just watching the local hack the thing up on the greasy table there was enough to make me not want any. But Pete would dig in and then take a couple of ciprofloxacin antibiotic pills afterward when he inevitably began to feel sick. I have eaten in restaurants in Jordan, Dubai, Cairo, and even the West Bank without getting sick, but Iraqi cooking just wasn't for me. I had a little charcoal grill, and you could buy frozen steaks at the bigger PXs, so if I wanted something special, I cooked it myself.

If nothing else, everyone had a laptop, and we all had internet access because every camp had its own satellite internet connection. We used to run around to the little Haji shops and buy bootleg DVDs for a dollar each. They weren't great quality, but they were cheap. You could also get real DVDs at the PX. I had every season of *Stargate* up to 2005 by the time I left. E-books weren't really a thing then, and paper books were too bulky to drag around with you, so I really missed reading. But you did the best you could to make the off time go by.

There weren't a lot of practical jokers on the teams. Everyone did their share of teasing and making jokes at each other's expense, but practical jokes usually meant messing with someone else's gear or food, and you just didn't do that. However, one of the smaller DFACs had a big chest freezer in the back where you could grab ice cream bars. The lid was heavy, and someone figured out that if you slammed it down with just the right amount of force, it sounded sort of like a mortar round going off outside. That trick got pulled every so often when there were a bunch of new guys around. Someone would slam the lid, and then all the guys who were used to it would laugh as several of the new guys jumped. Occasionally, someone would even bail off their chair, and then look sheepish as they stood up with everyone laughing. Black humor, but sort of a rite of passage in a way.

CHAPTER 50

Christmas in Iraq

Holidays were different in Iraq. The only two that we celebrated in any way were Thanksgiving and Christmas. The DFACs always put on a good meal for Thanksgiving. Sometimes the places I was assigned had their own DFAC, and sometimes we used the big military DFACS, but they were all good. Army food had changed a lot from what I was used to when I was on active duty. An Australian sergeant major once told me that the American food at the DFAC was so good that his guys were all gaining weight. He put them on PT twice a day to keep them in shape. I have to admit, the food was good, and the bigger DFACs had an insane amount of variety. There was a main line, a grill, a pasta bar, a taco bar, a salad bar, and a dessert bar. Thanksgiving dinner always had all the fixings.

I spent two Christmases in Iraq. They were the toughest holiday to be there for. I grew up in the northern United States, almost in Canada, and have lived over half my life since then in places where it snowed a lot. Iraq might get a few snow flurries occasionally, but nothing resembling real snow. Everything was the same uniform dust-brown color at Christmas as it was the rest of the year. A little cooler maybe, but still the desert.

People would put up lights to brighten things up. A couple of times I saw people paint a Santa Claus or Christmas tree on the 12-foot-high concrete T-walls that surrounded all our camps to protect them from blasts or attacks. But, if anything, it just made the place seem more forlorn. The amateurish bright red Santa looked out of place on the stark grey concrete surrounded by nothing but dirt and dust, but the thought was nice.

The DFACs were always festively decorated with Christmas trees and lights. You certainly couldn't fault them for the food and the way they did their best to help everyone get through a lonely Christmas. I know I am weird, but I actually like fruitcake, and they would have fruitcake at Christmas. I used to grab several pieces and take them back to my room to eat while I watched a movie. There was always a big dinner on Christmas day.

The mission tempo usually slowed down at Christmas because a lot of the clients would take R&R for the holidays. That meant we didn't have much to do, so everyone just sat around in their room. There was a whole camp of people around everyone, but it was lonelier than ever because there was nothing to keep you busy. Meals were the only time people really socialized all that much. But, it was fine and we all got through it. We'd all spent holidays away from home in the past when we were in the military, so it was nothing new.

Sex in the City

One of the things you quickly learn as an international security contractor is that people from other places often live by a very different set of standards than we do in America. This includes what their society finds normal and appropriate in their sex life. Iraq being the Wild West at that time, some of the things we ran into while I was working in the Green Zone probably shouldn't have been all that surprising. But they were.

CHAPTER 51

The Boy and the Filipino

There were a lot of Filipinos working in Iraq. They mostly held jobs in logistics, contracting, and administration. A few Filipinos were working as contracted static security guards, but most worked administrative and logistics jobs. Their government tried to block them from coming because of the danger, but thousands of them found ways around it because they could make so much more money there than at home. Since there was nowhere to go and their food was provided for them, most of the money they made could be sent back to the Philippines to support the families they left behind.

One of the Filipino guys working in admin at my employer's compound was openly gay. That wasn't a problem with anyone in the compound. He was easy to deal with and did his job, and no one cared what his sexual preference was. Unfortunately for him, he was the only gay person in the camp and the population of Type-A males in the compound didn't give him much of an opportunity to meet like-minded men. He tried flirting with some of our Kurdish static guards, but they weren't having any part of it. We finally had to counsel him that he made them uncomfortable, and that he might get hurt if he kept it up. When all else failed, he went looking for love outside the compound.

As with all Islamic countries, that I am aware of anyway, homosexuals are subject to widespread discrimination in Iraq. Same-sex marriage is illegal and gay people are frequently victims of familial honor killings because their families see them as a disgrace, and to vigilante attacks by enraged Muslims. He may or may have not known this, but if he did, I guess his physical needs overcame his common sense.

I was checking on the gate guards late one night when we heard the sound of running feet coming towards us. Since anything was possible, we all got ready to react to whatever might happen next. Imagine our surprise when the Filipino admin guy came pelting towards us. A short distance behind him were two Iraqi police officers. We let the Filipino guy pass, and he huddled behind us as we stopped the two police officers.

The Iraqis were quite upset and doing a lot of yelling and pointing at the terrified admin guy. We finally told him to go into the compound while we sorted things out. After a few minutes, our Kurdish guards told us the police were chasing the guy because they had caught him in an alley having oral sex with a 12-year-old Iraqi boy, and they wanted to arrest him. In this instance, arrest most likely meant beating him to death with their rifle butts.

This was a problem on many levels. For one, the Filipino was the employee of an American DoD contractor. For another, at that time, US contractors had immunity from prosecution by the Iraqi legal system. This was in place because the Iraqi legal system had largely consisted of Saddam's cronies and torture chambers for decades. There was only one thing to do ... we called the company's contract manager to come to the gate. We had no intention of turning him over to the enraged Iraqis, but we needed a legal and contractual interpretation to back it up.

He listened to all sides of the story, then determined that the Iraqi police had no jurisdiction over the Filipino admin guy, because he fell under the contractor immunity clause, so they could not arrest him. On the other hand, even though there was no avenue to charge him because he was not a US citizen, his conduct was a clear violation of US law which the company was bound to obey even in Iraq. Consequently, we assured the Iraqis that the Filipino admin guy would be on the first plane out of the country the next day.

The Iraqi police left grumbling, and we went to tell the admin guy to get packed and that he would be leaving in the morning. He was honestly shocked and confused. He could not understand what the problem was. The sex was consensual, and the Iraqi boy had been paid for his services. We told him that didn't matter, and that he was going home.

A security team took him to BIAP the next day and ensured he boarded a plane to Jordan. He had tickets all the way home to the Philippines, but in practice, he could go anywhere he wanted to once he was out of Iraq. A few days later he was emailing his former supervisor and asking when he could come back to work. He never did understand that getting caught by the police having sex in the street with a 12-year-old Iraqi boy was a problem.

In an odd twist to the story, it turned out that the 12-year-old boy was the son of a housekeeper working in the compound. There was some concern over how she might react to the entire incident, but other than a minor security concern it wasn't my problem. As it turned out, she never brought the matter up with anyone in the compound. That could be because it didn't bother her or that it was an embarrassment to the family and shouldn't be discussed. Sadly, it could also have been because her son did this regularly as a way to earn money the family needed to live. As future matters would confirm, underage prostitution was a lucrative business in the Green Zone.

CHAPTER 52

A Little Business on the Side

Jurisdiction in the Green Zone was a bit confusing. The US Air Force Security Forces, their version of MPs, patrolled the streets and tried to keep things under control. There were also Iraqi police around, but they only had jurisdiction over Iraqis and didn't seem to do much anyway. Army CID spent a lot of time policing the Army troops as well as investigating anything that seemed to be a threat to the security of the Green Zone. One day, CID paid me a visit.

My employer had a contract for maintaining some buildings critical to the Coalition war effort. They employed a lot of locals to do most of the grunt work, like cleaning and maintenance. CID had determined that one of their employees, an Iraqi woman who lived outside the Green Zone in Baghdad, was abusing her entry privileges and sneaking uncleared people into the Green Zone.

She would come into the Zone every morning for work and had the appropriate ID cards and permission letters to enable her to do that. Being an Iraqi, she primarily dealt with the Iraqi guards at the gate which allowed her to make "friends" and offer "encouragement" to cut her some slack from time to time. The CID guys explained that the slack she was enjoying enabled her to bring young girls, sometimes very young preteen girls, into the Green Zone.

There were a lot of Nepalese and other TCNs working in Iraq, both as security forces and as basic logistics laborers. Apparently, they had no age taboos, so the Iraqi woman was helping them scratch their itch with girls as young as 11 and 12. We verified who she was and when and where she normally worked. Shortly thereafter, she no longer showed up for work. Given the state of things, the only penalty she probably suffered was the loss of her access cards to enter Green Zone. With all the contractors living outside the wire in Baghdad and around BIAP, she probably didn't have too much difficulty finding a new housekeeping job, and sadly, probably even rebuilt her side business very quickly.

Peshmerga

The Kurdish word peshmerga *means "those who face death." It is what the Kurds call their standing military. It's actually more of a militia that protects the Kurdish people, but they are as well equipped as any militia in the region and a lot better trained. Although much of the world talks a great deal about the Palestinians, saying they have been deprived of their homeland, nobody worries much about the Kurds who have been in the same situation for centuries. Because what is ethnically Kurdistan sits at the point where the borders of Iraq, Iran, and Turkey meet, the Kurdish Peshmerga get plenty of action. Turkey regularly mounts military actions against ethnic Kurds in their territory, and Saddam used chemical weapons to kill as many as 5,000 men, women, and children in 1988. They are a strong people, tempered by a very harsh history. They are also trustworthy and capable, which is why they were employed as security contractors on two of my contracts in Iraq.*

CHAPTER 53

"Captain, Captain!"

Kurdistan has been around as a region since at least the 11th century, and the Kurdish people have been around a lot longer than that. They have a distinct ethnic identity and language, although Arabic, Turkish, Persian, and some other minor dialects are also spoken there. One thing that has been constant in the past few decades is that the United States has supported them while their regional neighbors have tried to wipe them out. As a result, they like Americans.

That, along with their martial competence, meant they were frequently employed by private security companies in Iraq. To say that Kurds and Iraqis do not like each other is an understatement. They hated each other enough that it was not safe for the Kurds working on our contracts with us to live out in the community, so they had to live in our camps with us. They would rotate a group down to work with us, and when some of them wanted to go back to Kurdistan to see their families, they would go back in a group, armed and ready to defend themselves along the way.

This isolation from the local community, and living in the same camp as the rest of us, made for a pretty close relationship between the American contractors and the Kurds, who we regularly referred to as the Pesh. That was especially true when I was doing convoy escort work. My regular vehicle crew was three or four Pesh, depending on whether or not our Lebanese interpreter, Casper, was riding with me. We worked and risked our lives together on every mission, and we trusted each other.

Although the Kurds were multilingual, fluently speaking Arabic, Turkish, and Persian along with Kurdish, English was not one of the languages most of them spoke. That made for some interesting moments when we were on a mission, especially in the heat of the moment. Since the vehicle crews were stable, with the same American and Pesh assigned to a specific truck, I could get to know their names. On the other hand, they didn't do well with American names, so they defaulted to calling us all "Captain." They would yell, "Captain, Captain!" which would be followed by a burst of Kurdish and broken English, accompanied by pointing and arm waving. It wasn't ideal, but it worked.

Sometimes the language differences were a great source of entertainment. On one contract we had both Nepalese Gurkhas and Kurdish guards working in the same compound. One day I came upon two of them trying valiantly to have a conversation about something. The official language of Nepal is Nepali, but there are actually a total of 123 languages spoken in the country. Most are offshoots of Hindi, Urdu, or Chinese, and none of them are English or Arabic. We've already talked about what the Kurds speak. So, what they ended up with was two people struggling to communicate in very poor broken English heavily accented by their native languages. I watched for a while but never figured out what they were trying to say to each other. As far as I could tell, they never did either, but no harm was done, and they both eventually went on their separate ways with a shrug and a smile.

The Kurds and the Americans took good care of each other most of the time. They lived at our camp with us, ate in our DFAC, and we made sure they were safe. As safe as the rest of us were, anyway. And they did whatever they could. We already knew they would fight by our side if it came to that. But they did little things, too.

Although it wasn't safe enough in Baghdad for our Kurdish teammates to live out in the community, it was generally safe enough for several of them at a time to make short trips out to local vendors, and much safer than it would have been for Americans. When we were sitting at the Abu Ghraib warehouse for hours waiting for some convoy to finally be loaded and ready to go, they would go to vendors outside the warehouse compound get food for us without us even asking them to. One particular guy would go to some little Iraqi bakery and bring me back fried egg sandwiches on fresh *samoon* bread. *Samoon* is an Iraqi bread shaped sort of like a canoe and baked in an outdoor brick oven. They were delicious, and the bread and eggs would still be warm when he'd give them to me. I tried to pay him for them, but he would never take any money. He would just smile and say, "For you, Captain," in his broken English.

They were good people. I wonder how many of them fought against Islamic State (ISIS) during the war in 2014 in Kurdistan. I'm sure most of them did. They weren't the kind of people to hide from a fight.

CHAPTER 54

Ali Baba!

If you have ever read *The Thousand and One Nights*, you probably know the story of Ali Baba and the Forty Thieves. In the story, Ali Baba is the hero who becomes wealthy by outsmarting 40 thieves. When I was in Iraq, Ali Baba was the name everyone called the Iraqi insurgents and terrorists who blew things up and kidnapped and beheaded people. If you spoke to either a Western soldier or contractor, or to a local, and said Ali Baba, everyone knew who you were talking about. How Ali Baba went from the hero of his story to the bad guy is lost in the endless sands of mil-speak, that enigmatic language of soldiers, airmen, and Marines.

One of the main ways we used the term was to describe the Iraqis who were secretly guerrilla fighters and who were infiltrating military bases or hiding in plain sight by blending in with the rest of the locals. After all, as Mao Zedong said, "The guerrilla must move amongst the people as a fish swims in the sea." This aspect of the war in Iraq was the main reason none of the companies I worked for ever employed locals as armed guards or members of any of the teams. We just couldn't trust them. We all felt it was much better, and safer, to employ Kurds and bring them down from Kurdistan and house them in our camps with us. There were too many verified reports of Iraqi guards turning on the people they were supposed to be protecting.

If anyone doubted the danger of blindly trusting Iraqis, the reality was amply demonstrated when five security contractors, four Americans and an Austrian, working for Crescent Security Group were abducted on November 16, 2006. They were stopped and taken at a fake checkpoint by a group of armed Iraqis that included men who worked with them as armed security contractors at the same company. At least three of them were executed and their headless bodies dumped in the desert. Consequently, we didn't trust Iraqis, but we did trust our Kurdish Peshmerga teammates.

Although our Kurds lived with us at our camp, they were still able to circulate outside the wire. Many of them had friends and even relatives living in the Baghdad areas, and this allowed them to get out of the camp when they felt like it. There was probably a degree of risk in their being outside the wire, especially if anyone out there figured out who they were and that they worked for the Americans, but I never heard of any of our guys disappearing or even having any serious problems. It also enabled them to do a little undercover checking into who was doing what in the community. That paid off for us one day.

Our convoys were never ready to go when we would get to the Abu Ghraib warehouse complex to pick them up, so we always had to sit around for an hour or more. We would hang out in the trucks or go talk to the Marines and other contractors, but as I mentioned earlier, our Kurds would wander around and talk to the locals. One day one of them came trotting up to me, his eyes wide and a look on his face that said something was wrong. His English wasn't much better than my Arabic, which wasn't good, so it took a minute to figure out what was up. After multiple repeats of "Captain, Captain," and "Ali Baba," I figured out he was trying to tell me he had seen a local inside the complex who he was certain was an insurgent.

I got the team leader and let him know what was up, and then we both went and found the Marine lieutenant who was our point of contact at the complex. He called over a couple of Marines, then we sent the Kurd off to find the guy again while we followed at a discreet distance. We told him to go say something to the guy when he saw him, and the Marines would swoop in and grab him. It worked like a charm, and Ali Baba was soon being frog-marched off to a small room for a serious conversation. Our Pesh basked in the praise we gave him for his minute of fame, and then we all went back to what we were doing before the excitement started.

The possibility of an insurgent trying to get access to the warehouse complex was very real. The place was packed to overflowing with all sorts of weapons, medical supplies, military equipment, and even explosives. It would have been a guerrilla's dream. They had tried to use conventional tactics to attack the place before, but it was too much of a hard target. Infiltrating was the next logical step, and with all the local labor employed there, sneaking someone in would be possible if not easy. The locals were vetted before being given access, but in a place like Iraq security was a difficult thing to maintain. Whatever the story on how the guy got access, Ali Baba didn't get his way thanks to a Pesh fighter who didn't want anything bad to happen to his friends and allies.

CHAPTER 55

Pesh Just Like to Shoot Guns

Shooting guns is a favorite pastime in the Middle East, especially in Iraq. Guns are shot off for just about any occasion you can think of. Weddings, winning a sports event, celebrating something, and even funerals seem to involve shooting guns up into the air. When I lived at one of the company villas in Bagdad, there were small piles of spent bullets on the sidewalk in front of the house every morning. Bullets that had fallen out of the air after being shot up from somewhere.

Our Kurdish Pesh were perhaps a little more disciplined than the Iraqis surrounding us, but they liked to shoot their guns, too. This was especially true when we were on missions. They went through an incredible amount of ammunition while out on missions. It was a running joke among us Americans. But, as I mention elsewhere in this book, that was their job. When a convoy was attacked, they were supposed to shoot while we were supposed to drive. Sometimes they got a little carried away, like the time my tail gunner fired a warning shot at a British Army convoy that he thought was too close behind us. That could have been a Bad Thing. Fortunately, it turned out okay.

The Kurds working with us had received more training than the average Iraqi, first as Peshmerga in Kurdistan, then with our own instructors. They were trained in operations, marksmanship, how to maintain their weapons, and gun safety. The safety part didn't always stick.

I had what, at the time, felt like a near-death experience while we were sitting just outside the ECP for a small US base just outside of Tikrit. I don't even recall what we were waiting for, just one of the hurry-up-and-wait scenarios we lived every week. I was in the cab of my truck parked just behind one of the other trucks. Two of the Pesh were in the back of the other truck, including one that I used to joke around with a lot. He was sitting behind the PKM 7.62mm machine gun mounted in the back of the truck. He looked at me and grinned as he grabbed the machine gun and pretended to swing it around. As he did so he apparently pulled the trigger. There was a loud report as several rounds went into the dirt just to the right of the front tire of my truck. He looked shocked and embarrassed as I raised my eyebrows and gave him a look that clearly said, "WTF?!"

He let go of the gun like it was on fire and put his hands up in front of him in a gesture that clearly said he was as surprised as I was. An American soldier came around the side of the wall fronting the base to see what was going on, but there was nothing to see by then, so he walked off without saying anything. I wasn't more than 20 feet from the muzzle of that very efficient killing machine when it went off. To this day I can still imagine what would have happened had it been pointed toward me when that goof-off Kurd hit the trigger. It still gives me chills.

Improvised Explosive Devices

IEDs caused a lot of casualties among everyone in Iraq. Coalition troops, contractors, and Iraqi civilians all ended up dead and wounded by insurgent IEDs. I saw and experienced it personally on multiple occasions. IEDs were not discriminatory about who they wounded and killed, and I have no doubt they killed and wounded more of their fellow Iraqis than Westerners. But they were effective, and they became more effective as the war progressed and the insurgents became more sophisticated in their tactics and the types of IEDs they employed.

They started out relatively crude. Early versions were explosives from artillery rounds buried by the side of the road with a detonator. They were often hardwired, with the wires running out to a hiding place where the operator could see the road. When the target approached, they would detonate the IED with a switch or sometimes by just touching two wires together. Very crude and not all that reliable. It also relied on the hand/eye coordination of the person detonating it to time it to hit the intended target: something that was difficult to do well, and that probably caused a lot of civilian casualties.

Later they used cell phones, and even garage door openers to detonate the IEDs. The IEDs themselves went from crude bombs using explosives from artillery shells to EFPs (explosively formed penetrators) that worked like shaped charges and would cut right through heavy vehicle armor. They would go through the armor in up-armored SUVs like a hot knife through butter.

The biggest frustration surrounding IEDs was that there was no way to fight back. All you could do was drive along and hope you didn't get hit. And if you spent any significant amount of time on the road at all, you knew you were going to get hit sooner or later. My teams were targeted four times while I was in Iraq, three of which directly targeted my vehicle. I was lucky beyond words that I was never caught in the primary blast radius of the device. Part of that luck was because my encounters were in 2004 to early 2006, and the IEDs that targeted my vehicle weren't all that sophisticated yet. Another team working with me was hit by an EFP in late 2006 with devastating results which I will cover later.

Whether they were simple or sophisticated, IEDs killed and maimed more American troops and contractors than any other single threat in Iraq. They were the great equalizer for the Iraqis that addressed the imbalance in firepower and technology they suffered in fighting the Coalition. They were cheap, relatively easy to assemble, and devastatingly effective. I attended multiple memorial services for contractors and troops killed by IEDs while I was in Iraq. I got very used to the sound of bagpipes that were frequently played at contractor memorials.

CHAPTER 56

The Road to Haditha Dam

When my PSD team was stationed at Firebase Laramore-Matthews at Bayji in 2004, we received a mission to conduct a recce out to Haditha Dam which gave me my first experience with an IED. The client was getting ready to start a project there, and we needed to get familiar with the route, look for choke points and high-risk areas, and just get a feel for the area in general. Like a close protection advance team. Since we wouldn't have any clients with us, we all loaded up in the team's two soft-skin Suburbans.

We went down Route 1 to Route 19 southwest toward Haditha. Route 19 went straight as a ruler out across the Iraqi desert. You could see for miles in every direction so the bad guys could see us coming from a long way off. It was a divided highway with two lanes in each direction. That fact would very shortly save us.

I was driving the lead vehicle and our Nepalese team members were in the second vehicle. I had just pulled into the left lane to pass a bus full of Iraqis when the IED went off. Most of the blast caught the bus which swerved off the road. Our second vehicle was behind me and wasn't as protected by the bus as we were, so it caught some metal and roadside stones from the explosion. Fortunately, all it did was put some stars across the windshield. As per PSD doctrine, once we saw that the second vehicle was not immobilized, we kept going and didn't bother checking out the damage until we reached a secure location. We had no way of knowing how the civilians in the bus fared.

The rest of the mission was run with the knowledge that Ali Baba, as the bad guys were universally called, was out there and watching for targets of opportunity. We weren't attacked again on that trip, but you can be sure that we gave anything that even looked remotely suspicious a wide berth. That included roadside trash, piles of rocks, and dead animal carcasses. The insurgents had been known to hide IEDs in all of those places. The potential locations that worried me the most were culverts that ran under the road. Stuffing one of them with explosives and detonating them as we drove over it would be devastating. Fortunately, we didn't encounter anything like that.

CHAPTER 57

The Wreck, the Wedding, and the Marine

When I was doing convoy escort out of the Abu Ghraib warehouse, we worked with a young Marine lieutenant who was our contact there. He was a good guy who used to keep us supplied with a few extras like frag and smoke grenades that weren't easy to come by for contractors. Being a Marine, he was bored just hanging around the warehouse all day and he wanted to get out on the road and make a run with us. With an okay from my team leader, I let him ride along with me one day.

I was running mid-convoy instead of my usual trail position, and he was in the passenger seat enjoying the ride and using a silicone cloth to wipe the dust off his MP5. Don't ask me why he had an MP5 instead of an M4, but that's what he had. We were driving down a busy divided highway on the outskirts of Baghdad when I noticed a wrecked SUV lying on its side to our left in the dirt dividing the two sides of the highway. Something about it didn't look right to me. It was too shiny, too clean to have been sitting there very long. Almost as if it had been dropped there recently.

It's always a good idea to act on your instincts, and I acted on mine. I cranked the wheel and moved from the left lane to the right lane just as the IED that was in the wreck exploded. Apparently, it wasn't a directional bomb, so it blew out across both lanes going in each direction. The Marine in the cab with me yelled something as I instinctively ducked. Fortunately for us, the blast and most of the flying debris missed us, and as far as we could tell, our truck only had a few new dings and scratches in it when we checked it later.

An Iraqi wedding party coming the other direction wasn't so fortunate. Iraqis cover their cars with flowers when they are in a wedding procession. Several of the guys in the last vehicles later recalled seeing a cloud of flowers flying through the air as the explosion caught the procession. Rough way to start a marriage. As for the Marine lieutenant who was riding with me, he got a little action and a new story to tell when he got back to the warehouse complex. For us, it was just another convoy. My team leader joked that he'd been around for so many IEDs that one more, and he'd win a set of steak knives. Black humor was always a good coping mechanism. He also blamed himself for not noticing that the wreck didn't look right and warning everyone to give it a wide berth. We told him not to worry about it, it's impossible to catch everything.

CHAPTER 58

The Convoy

My third IED experience happened when we were escorting a big convoy with over a dozen trucks, so three teams were running with it. We were on our way back to Baghdad, and the trucks were all empty, having unloaded everything at some Iraqi Army base, but we kept them in the convoy for the return trip. I was about two-thirds of the way back in the line and had just come up over a hill so I could look down the road and see the convoy spread out in front of me. We were passing through a busy built-up area that must have been a village with a gas station and store on both sides of the road. Suddenly, I saw an explosion towards the front of the convoy, a short way past the built-up area. My truck was still in the built-up area, so there was a lot of traffic and pedestrians around us. Everyone was looking down the road toward where the explosion had been. People are the same whether they are in Iraq or the US.

I was driving, but I knew the Kurds were watching what was going on around us. Nevertheless, I picked my M4 up from where it rested between the seats and put it across in front of me with the muzzle out the window. There was no way to determine if it was just a simple IED attack, or if the IED was the trigger for a complex ambush attack. Cars were starting to crowd out onto the road where there was a chance they would get in between the convoy vehicles. It was probably innocent, but the Kurds fired a few warning shots into the road to keep them back. The locals got the message and kept their distance. The last thing we needed were cars filled with unknown locals interspersed between the trucks in the convoy.

The convoy kept moving and we were soon past the spot. The explosion had missed the vehicles, so everyone kept moving. There had been just one explosion, and no one seemed to be shooting at us, so we decided it was an isolated attack. Since the convoy had already delivered its cargo, we determined it would be safer to tell the truck drivers they could go on their way if they wanted to, instead of staying in the convoy. Unsurprisingly, they all took off on their own since that was safer for them than staying in a convoy that was an obvious target for IEDs and potentially other types of attacks. It was safer for us, too, because without the trucks to shepherd, we could go faster and break up into teams that wouldn't attract as much attention. Since no one seemed to have suffered any visible damage, that one went into the win column for us and a loss for the insurgents. We weren't always that lucky.

CHAPTER 59

Death from Above

Whoever set up the last IED that directly targeted my vehicle showed a little more ingenuity than usual. We were somewhere just outside of Baghdad; all the convoys seem to run together after a while especially when you're the last vehicle. It's like you never really know where you are, you just follow the vehicle in front of you, the whole while watching out for potential threats coming up from behind you. The only sure way to know where you are is the notification coming across the radio from the first vehicle. Anyway, it was an expressway with the usual overpasses. I do remember that we didn't have any trucks with us at the time so we must have been heading back to camp at the end of a run.

As we approached an overpass, I noticed two Iraqis standing on the little grassy slope on the edge of the road that went over the expressway. They were both just standing there leaning on rakes or shovels and watching our gun trucks go by. It seemed odd to me because there were just the two guys. No service truck and no other workers. They didn't have vests on or anything, not that that meant anything in Iraq. I got that feeling again that something wasn't right. The one that it usually isn't a good idea to ignore.

It was a standard tactic to try never to come out from under the other side of an overpass in the same lane you were in when you went in under it. There had been cases of people waiting on the overpass to shoot down at vehicles because most up-armored SUVs don't have any armor in the roof. Sometimes they would drop a grenade tied to a string so it would stop falling at windshield level before it blew up. Switching lanes under the overpass might throw an ambusher off. The expressway had three lanes in each direction, and I went from the right lane to the far-left lane. I remember going around one of those little white Toyota Hilux pickup trucks that are all over the Mideast. Just as I got to the far-left lane under the bridge, the IED went off. It had been mounted up under the far-right edge of the overpass, probably with an aimed charge pointing down onto the road. Pretty creative, really.

I'm guessing the two guys standing by the overpass triggered it with a phone or garage door opener, but they weren't expecting me to change lanes like I did. The way it worked out, the IED mostly missed us, but it hit the little white truck with the two Iraqis in it pretty hard. There was a lot of smoke and dust so I couldn't see much, but I had a fleeting impression of the truck stopped in the middle of the lane with the doors open. My ears were ringing, but I thought I heard a few gunshots, which my Kurds must have heard too because they opened up with their AKs. I had no idea if they actually saw anyone shooting at us or if they started shooting just in case. We all just wanted to survive another day.

I got on the radio to tell the rest of the team that we'd been hit with an IED and that I thought we were taking fire. I hit the gas and closed up with the team, which had sped up to get out of the ambush area and then stopped about a klick up the road. As I pulled up to them, everybody got out laughing and clapping their hands. Being the sensitive guys that they were, they all laughed and said they thought I'd bought it that time for sure. They also thought my radio call under pressure had been very entertaining. I will admit my voice may have been an octave or so higher, but I didn't think it was *that* funny.

As it turned out, my tail gunner had caught a small piece of shrapnel in the leg and there were a few dings in the truck. We patched him up and radioed ahead to have a medical team waiting for us when we reached the perimeter of the secure area near BIAP where our camp was. A team from our company and an Army medical team were there waiting for us and checked him over. The medic said he thought there was probably a small piece of metal in his leg, but it wasn't worth the pain and effort to dig it out. Since he didn't need any additional treatment, we all went back to camp where I got to tell my story several times to different people.

A couple of the senior guys came and checked the truck out and told me how lucky I was. As if I didn't know. It was one of those close calls that provided plenty of excitement with no harm being done, at least not to us. I'm sure the two Iraqis in the little pickup truck felt differently. It was just another example of how indiscriminate weapons like IEDs are. I had seen it with the bus and the wedding party from the previous IED attacks, but I'll never forget that little truck sitting there with the doors open.

CHAPTER 60

Arty Rounds on Haifa Street

We were coming back from a very long mission escorting a large convoy to an Iraqi Army base out on the Syrian border. We had three full teams totaling 12 trucks, but no semi-trucks with us. We'd delivered the convoy trucks and spent the night in the barracks at the base where the Iraqi Army cooks had prepared a meal for us. They must have been cooking out of a makeshift kitchen because the base DFAC had been destroyed in a mortar attack a couple of weeks earlier. We had passed it as we traveled through the base, and no one was going to be preparing meals there for a long time. The Kurds had loved the food, but the rest of us weren't ready to trust our health to Iraqi Army cooks, so we had eaten nothing but MREs for a few days. It was after dark and we'd been on the road all day coming home, so we were looking forward to getting back to camp to relax and get something decent to eat.

We were on Haifa Street, a main road that runs through Baghdad roughly parallel to the Tigris River, when we were stopped by a US Army patrol. They said there was an IED in the road ahead of us and we had to wait for EOD to get there to clear it. They had no idea how long it would be before we could proceed.

So, there we were, 12 stationary trucks spread out down the road in the dark close to an Army patrol. Just sitting there like the perfect target. We got out of the trucks figuring that if anything happened it was better to be on foot so we could at least take cover than to be sitting in a stationary vehicle. There were buildings close to the road on one side, and we could hear people moving around them on the street and in the alleys, but the streetlights where I was stopped were out so I couldn't see who they were or what they were doing. We had a quick meeting to discuss our options. Basically, we could either try to go around the problem by finding our way through the maze of side streets where anything could happen, or we could sit there for who knew how long waiting while anything could happen.

There was a third option. We could persuade the Army to let us go by the IED so we could get the hell out of there. After all, we were used to IEDs, and as long as we knew where it was, we could avoid it. Probably. We floated the idea to the Army, and after some persuasion, they agreed we could proceed.

They explained that the IED was three 152mm Russian artillery shells wired together and sitting on the side of the road just off the northbound side of the divided road. Haifa Street actually runs more NW to SE, but you get the idea. We were advised to turn off our radios and cell phones to reduce the risk of accidentally detonating the IED, which we willingly did. Then we mounted up and pulled ahead.

Our trucks had armored shutters over the side windows. They could open up to an extent and had a slit you could look or shoot through, as the situation called for. The IED was on the side of the road in the northbound lane, and we were heading south so we figured if we got as far to the right as we could we'd have four lanes and the center divider between us and it. The smart thing to do would have been to lean well back behind the armored shutter, but where's the fun in that? We were little more than a bunch of overgrown boys, and everyone wanted to see the IED, so I leaned forward and peeked around the edge of the shutter.

There was a streetlight not too far away and I could just make out the IED sitting there on the side of the road. Everything around it was covered in concrete so the guys who put it there couldn't bury it, and it didn't look like any attempt had been made to hide it. I could see what looked like three artillery shells standing on their ends all wired together.

It seemed odd that they hadn't tried to hide it somehow, but maybe the insurgents were counting on the fact that American patrols came that way every night and wouldn't see it in the dim conditions. The thought even crossed my mind that maybe it wasn't even intended to be a serious IED, but it was bait to get an American EOD team out there so they could be shot at. But if that was the case, why hadn't the presence of the Army patrol or even us being there triggered the ambush? It was a mystery then and remains one to me to this day. Whatever the circumstances of it being there were, we got past it with nothing happening and went on our way back to camp with one more story to tell.

CHAPTER 61

Explosively Formed Penetrators

By 2006, IEDs in Iraq had become much more sophisticated. They had gone from a few artillery shells wired together with a cell phone to set them off, to simple but effective shaped charges called explosively formed penetrators (EFP) that could penetrate medium and heavy armor. The intelligence community said that the original EFPs were provided by Iran, who also trained local insurgents how to build their own. An EFP was essentially a concave copper plate with an explosive-filled cavity behind it. The explosives detonate, superheating the copper and turning it into a molten projectile that can punch through almost anything. The military had the equipment to help them defeat this type of IED and jammers that blocked the signal for command-detonated versions. Private security companies had nothing to defend themselves with. All we could do was hope we didn't get hit with one.

That luck ran out in the summer of 2006 for a team I worked with but wasn't a member of. The tempo of combat and insurgent attacks had stepped up throughout Iraq. I was the country security manager for a reconstruction contractor that had its primary camp in the Green Zone but had other camps throughout Iraq. Along with our own private security managers, we had a couple of security companies contracted to provide PSD teams to move the various engineers and construction managers around Iraq.

I reviewed and signed off on proposed movements for the following day and week, so I knew the team would be going out the next morning on a run to a job site they had been to before. Along with their regular team, they would be taking the new interpreter we had just hired a couple of days before. His name was Mohammad, and he was the cousin of one of our housekeepers. He was a good kid with excellent English skills. We issued him some equipment and he got some basic training for how to not be in the way during a PSD movement. Because he was the interpreter for the security team, he rode in one of the up-armored security vehicles rather than in the B6 with the clients. The team departed camp at 0700. It was his first mission.

At around 0830 I got a phone call from the operation center. I was informed the team had been hit by an IED. The clients were safe, but the team had suffered two killed in action and one wounded. Mohammad had been riding in the back seat behind the driver. He and the South African team member on the passenger side of the back seat had been killed. The team medic had worked on Mohammad and got his breathing started a couple of times, but his injuries were too severe, and he was dead by the time the military medevac got there. The South African in the front passenger seat had been seriously wounded and died a day later. Miraculously, the driver only had a tiny scratch on his hand. The seat under his legs and the hydration pack he was wearing were both full of holes from flying splinters. The gunner riding in the very back of the SUV was not injured.

The vehicle was heavily damaged and was taken to a base for evaluation of the blast effects. The plasma created by the molten copper had cut holes through the armor plate that were smooth enough to have been done with a cutting torch. It was a hot summer day, so all the blood-soaked upholstery in the seats had been torn out so it wouldn't start smelling in the heat. It was returned to us a few days later after being evaluated. Mohammad's torn and bloody equipment was returned to us the same day, and we burned it.

The clients that had been riding in the B6 vehicle were pretty shook up. They'd been safe because the EFP hadn't targeted the vehicle they were in. If it had, the molten jet of copper would probably have penetrated it, even though it was more heavily armored than the up-armored Suburban had been. They probably knew that. The team had followed SOP and gotten the client's vehicle out of the area while the rest of the team had tried to care for their wounded and protect them until the Army arrived.

That night, one of the clients who had been on the run recorded a video talking about the episode and his feelings. I remember thinking that he looked like a broken man, and I considered recommending that he be sent out of the country for a break if he didn't snap out of it. Eventually, he got over the shock and continued to work on the project, but no one would have blamed him if he had left. He was an engineer who had come to Iraq to rebuild the country's power infrastructure. He wasn't a soldier or a security contractor.

The armor inserts in the vehicle, that had done well protecting team members from small arms and even the worst effects of near misses with conventional IEDs, had not even slowed down the molten copper from the EFP. The official figures said that 195 American service members were killed and close to 900 wounded by EFPs from July 2005 to November 2011. As usual, there are no accurate figures for contractors. The stakes had definitely gone up.

The insurgents' employment of EFPs meant there was really no effective protection for contractors from IEDs. The holes the molten copper made through armor plate weren't even jagged and it didn't deform the plate. It just cut a smooth hole right through it. If you were in its path when it shot out of the device, it would go through you, too. And the worst thing about it was that there was no way to fight back. You just rode down the road and hoped for the best.

The reality of the EFP didn't change operations. The US government still expected reconstruction contractors to complete their contracted projects, and the contractors still expected us to provide the security necessary for them to do that. PSD teams still moved people around, and convoy escorts still made sure critical material got where it needed to go.

Working with Expats

An inescapable aspect of doing international security contracting is working with expatriates, or expats, for short. Technically, an expat is anyone living outside their own country, but when discussing any place Americans are working, the US State Department defines expats as Americans, and sometimes Westerners like Brits, who live in another country. Everyone else, meaning folks from places like South America, Asia, or Africa, are classified as third-country nationals or TCNs, meaning they are not from the United States or the host country, but from a third country.

American expats are an interesting breed. They want to work in a less-structured environment than they could find in the US. They like adventure and, in another age, they might have been pioneers and adventurers. They also like money, and believe me, expats get paid very well when working on international development contracts for the US government. I saw it in Iraq, and I would see it over and over throughout my career in international security.

But all their independence makes them a bit eccentric, and sometimes difficult to work with, which is probably one of the reasons they choose to work in developing nations in the first place, since working in the American corporate world requires a certain level of self-discipline and social competence. Don't get me wrong, most of them are great people, and I enjoyed working with them, but they are very independent, and some have interesting personalities and habits. That resulted in some odd situations over the years I was in Iraq. Some of it was simple stuff, like resisting wearing their body armor on field outings or trying to get over by wearing the vests but taking out the rigid bulletproof plates because they were too heavy. Other times, the situations were like something out of a TV show.

CHAPTER 62

Vacation with the Family, or One of Them Anyway

Employers generally require employees to fill out an emergency contact form, particularly in dangerous environments like Iraq, and the company I was doing security for in 2006 was no exception. Their expat employees working in Iraq had a contract that allowed them 14 days of R&R for every 75 days they were in-country. They could leave Iraq and go home to visit family or go on a vacation somewhere to escape the stress of working in a conflict zone and recharge their batteries. So, when one of their employees, we'll call him Arthur, went out on R&R his emergency contact form was on file.

A couple of days after he flew out, Arthur called one of his coworkers to let him know that he had been arrested in Ghana, Africa, because he'd hit and killed a pedestrian with his car. Unlike the United States, in Africa, you are considered guilty unless you can prove your innocence, and he had been arrested on charges of murder even though it had been an accident. This was not unusual there, and we were confident that the US Embassy and a local lawyer could get him out of it.

In the meantime, being in charge of security, I went to HR (Human Resources) and got his emergency contact form so I could inform his family back in the States what was going on. I assumed his family knew he was in Africa and knew why he had gone there. When I called the number on the form someone who sounded like a teenage girl answered the phone, so I asked her to get her mother. When Arthur's wife got on the line, I explained the situation to her and reassured her we would get it worked out.

I was met with complete silence. Intuition told me something wasn't right, so I asked if she knew her husband was in Ghana. She said, no. So, I said, "You didn't even know he was on R&R, did you?" Again, she said no. I gave her the number to my employer's HR department and told her she could contact them as the situation progressed.

Eventually, Arthur was released and returned to work in Iraq. When the details of the episode came out it turned out that he had a home with a wife and family in Ghana as well as in the United States. When he got back, he came to see me and started to berate me for calling his wife in the United States. I quickly told him don't even go there, and that we had used the contact information he provided. That was the end of the conversation. How the conversation went between him and his wife in the US, I neither found out nor cared but could well imagine.

CHAPTER 63

Demon Rum in the Green Zone

One summer night in 2006 I awoke in my hooch to the sound of a huge volume of small arms fire and someone pounding on my door. It was one of my security managers telling me he thought the insurgents were attacking the checkpoints at the entrances to the Green Zone. I got moving and told him to get a head count of everyone who lived in the compound. As I moved through the compound trying to get a handle on the situation, I could hear objects hitting the ground. I immediately realized they were probably bullets coming down after being shot up into the air.

Falling bullets can be almost as dangerous as bullets that have been shot at you. We had a man hit and wounded by a falling bullet the year before at Camp Victory and I knew they could go through the roofs of the prefab rooms where people slept, so I ordered all the residents of the compound who lived in the prefab trailers to go into the bunkers or one of the several permanent buildings where the offices were.

Since the compound was in the Green Zone, the expats working and living there could go out to restaurants and friends' camps as long as they were back by the midnight curfew. It was late and everyone was accounted for except one expat, we'll call him John.

Despite all military and government contractors being subject to General Order Number 1, which prohibited the possession of alcohol in Iraq, there was plenty of booze available, and John took advantage of that regularly. In fact, John drank heavily. Much more heavily than anyone in a conflict zone should ever drink.

To his credit, John answered his phone right away when we called him and told us where he was. He was obviously inebriated, so we told him to stay where he was, and that we would send a security team over to collect him and the vehicle he was using. He refused to wait, insisting that he could just drive himself back through the Green Zone to the compound. Even though the Green Zone wasn't all that large, we told him to stay where he was and sent the team to collect him. We didn't need him getting hurt while out on his own and drunk.

When the team arrived at the location John had given us, he had already left. Since he wasn't back yet I called him again. He answered and told me he was a "little bit lost." I asked him to describe what he was seeing so I could figure out where he was. He told me he could see the rear end of a tank and he was about to go past it.

The only tanks in the Green Zone were at the exit points where the streets went outside the wire and into Baghdad. Since no one cared if you left the area, the exit points were not as heavily guarded or blocked with barriers as the entrance checkpoints. To prevent bad guys from coming in through the exit point, each one had an M1 Abrams tank sitting there with its main gun pointing out into the city in the direction anyone trying to enter the Green Zone through the exit point would be coming from. But there was nothing to prevent anyone from just driving past it on their way out, and no one would stop them.

John was about to drive past that tank and out into Baghdad. Not a good thing at the best of times, and even less good with him drunk and all the shooting going on. I forcefully told him to stop immediately and pull over, then sent the security team to find him. They did, and John was on a plane home the next day.

Like all the expat engineers working in Iraq, John made a lot of money. It was too bad that he couldn't manage to stay sober for 75 days at a time. His inability to do so was a risk in a place like Iraq, not only to himself but to the people around him. This was evidenced by the fact that I had one of my security teams running around in the night looking for him with bullets falling out of the sky. His employer, on my recommendation, agreed and he lost his job on the grounds that he had violated curfew and put others at risk by being drunk during an emergency. Demon rum had cost him a six-figure-a-year job.

As it turned out, the Iraqis had won a game in the soccer World Cup competition and most of the shooting was celebratory fire. Iraqis like to shoot their guns in the air a lot. But even though there was apparently no deliberate attack on the checkpoints, more than a few locals took the opportunity to put some fire in that direction under the cover of all the shooting going on. There were also plenty of bullets falling into the camp as they came back down that night, as evidenced by my hearing objects hitting the ground around me in the compound. A bullet that is shot up into the air will come back to Earth at around 150 miles per hour. More than enough to inflict a wound and even cause death if it hits someone in the right place. Fortunately, the guy who had been wounded the year before had been hit in the top of his butt cheek. Of the ones that fell in the compound that night, one bullet penetrated the roof in one of the sleeping quarters right over an unoccupied bed, and another went through the hood of a vehicle in the motor pool. Some celebration.

CHAPTER 64

A Difference in Perspective

Security contractors went to Iraq for a lot of different reasons. Some missed being in the military. Some of them were looking for adventure. Some were there for the money … a lot were there for the money. Some of them just liked to fight and wanted to make their living carrying a gun. All of them came from some form of martial background. Most were prior military, though a few were former police SWAT types. All of them were used to taking orders and liked a certain amount of structure in their lives.

By contrast, expats who went to Iraq for jobs in engineering, construction management, or contract administration were a very different breed. Most of them did what they did for the money, and they made even more money than security contractors did. Added to the direct income was the fact that living in out-of-the-way countries was a lot cheaper than living in the US, so they got to keep more of their money. Living in Iraq was free, since their living arrangements were provided by their employer or the government.

All of them liked an environment where people weren't always telling them what to do. Doing the same kind of work they were doing in Iraq in the United States or Europe would have been far too structured for them. They wanted the freedom to do things their way. The opportunity to live somewhere exotic was a bonus.

Most expats got along well enough with the security teams. They knew the security contractors would risk their lives to protect them, if for no other reason than just because it was their job. A few resisted, like the ones who tried to get away with no plates in their body armor. Some of them also resented our authority over them when they were out in the field, or even if there was a security incident that affected the compound or the surrounding area. There were also a few who actively hated us. One guy regularly called me the Gestapo, but he wasn't easy to get along with in general. The person in the next room said he could hear the guy yelling at his wife on the phone at night. One or two claimed they were actually afraid of us because we carried guns. I told them so did the bad guys, so they should be glad we did too.

But we also had to understand that some of them had been working in third-world countries for longer than some of the security guys had been alive. The politically correct term these days is developing nations, although I never saw a whole lot of development going on in most of the places I worked. They were used to being the big shots on projects, and a part of their independent streak was that they didn't like to take orders, and there were times we had to give them orders. Once there was a suspected VBIED discovered sitting right next to the compound. We needed to evacuate all the buildings near it, and we didn't have time to ask them nicely. We just walked in and told everyone to get out now and go to the far side of the compound. Sometimes they would argue or demand to know why they had to do something, but in this case, they knew how dangerous a VBIED was, some of them had seen the results personally, so no one gave us any argument. The Army came and shot one of the car windows out, then brought in one of their little tracked robots to drop a thermite grenade into the car and burn it to scrap. Most people don't know that bombs don't usually explode when the vehicle is burned, it takes a detonator to go off to initiate the explosion. We never heard anything more about it, so I guess it was a false alarm, but it isn't the sort of warning you ignore.

What some of them didn't consider was that, even though it is dangerous working in the places they were used to, most parts of Africa, South America, or Asia are dangerous because of crime and cartels. Iraq was an active conflict zone where every American had a big bullseye painted on them. The security contractors, with their military backgrounds, were used to taking and giving orders. Security companies work very much on a military model. There weren't any formations and no saluting, but there was a clear command structure and when you were on a mission, you gave and followed orders. Very few of the expat contractors, the engineers and admin types, had ever been in the military, and it showed. They questioned everything and wanted to know the reason behind something before they would consider following any orders or policies.

Sometimes the differences in our outlooks took me by surprise. I was eating lunch at one of the big DFACs with some of the clients one day when a security team from another company came in and sat down. One of the guys was huge. He had to be at least 6'4" and well over 250 pounds. He obviously spent a lot of time in the gym.

As I sat there looking at him, I was thinking of being on a team with him. The thought that ran through my mind was, "Man, he'd be a real pain to have to pull out of a disabled vehicle if he was injured." The expat sitting next to me was an older woman who was part of the client's admin team. A really nice lady who got along well with the security types. As I sat thinking she suddenly spoke up and said, "Boy, now he'd be able to get me out of a burning vehicle fast." I looked at her and chuckled, and then told her I was just thinking how much work it'd be to get *him* out of a burning vehicle.

At first, I was surprised by her comment because it just hadn't occurred to me. Our perspectives were the direct opposites of each other. I thought in terms of being responsible for saving someone, and she thought in terms of being saved. There was nothing wrong with either perspective, they were just different. The key to success was for everyone to do their best to see things from each other's perspective.

Our job was to keep the clients safe, although there was no way to actually guarantee that. Even forcing them to stay on the protected compounds and military bases wasn't a guarantee. Plenty of people were killed and injured by mortar rounds, rockets, various types of bombs, and the occasional shooting on the bases and in the Green Zone. Several Filipino contractors were killed on Camp Liberty, right outside the door to the PX, by a mortar round one day. I was there a few days later and saw the divot in the paving stones and the shrapnel tears on a nearby metal light pole. But they were safer inside the wire than outside it.

The clients were there because they had contracts to build things like schools, water treatment plants, and police stations in Iraq for the US government. If they didn't make trips outside the wire, with all the associated risks, they couldn't do their jobs and there was no point in them even being in Iraq. Our job was to facilitate their work, not prevent it. Most of the time we all did our jobs in relative harmony, or at least strained tolerance, although there were a few times when personalities and perspectives combined to boil over into confrontations. One incident involved a client, we'll call him Hank, and a security contractor we'll call Wes. It centered on the usual dispute over the client trying to get away with taking the armor plates out of his plate carrier vest. In all fairness, neither of them got along well with anybody else, so it was more or less inevitable that they would clash eventually.

Hank showed up for a PSD ride between two bases, and Wes did the usual check to ensure everyone had their plates in. Hank had taken his plates out, so Wes told him he wasn't allowed to get in the vehicle. I have to say that I honestly do not understand why some of the clients tried to get away with taking their plates out. They really weren't that uncomfortable, but then, we were used to wearing them on multiple missions every week. At any rate, Hank flashed and got aggressive with Wes, who failed completely to de-escalate the situation, and the two got into a shoving match. They both lost their jobs over it.

Frankly, we all knew the clients could be testy at times. It was up to us to be professional no matter the situation. Years later, while working in Afghanistan, I had a woman get within a couple of inches of my face and scream at me because I wouldn't let her walk down the street in Kabul to a shop to buy a Snickers bar. I guess she really wanted a Snickers bar. I managed to stay calm and tell her the answer was no. The secret is realizing that it's nothing personal, the clients are just frustrated and stressed by the circumstances, and we are sometimes a convenient target to let it out on. It's sort of like being a cop that way.

Exploring

One aspect of being in Iraq for a couple of years was the opportunity to explore the place. This was especially fun around Baghdad since Saddam had spared no expense in feeding his ego by building all sorts of things like palaces, monuments, parade grounds, and even a Flintstones-style village. He also liked to collect things like fighter planes and tanks. When we were off duty for a day or two, we often took the opportunity to see the sights, especially in the early days after the invasion when the Iraqi government was non-existent and there was no one controlling access to anything.

Unlike most of the reconstruction contractors, security contractors usually didn't have anyone telling them where they could go and where was off-limits. Of course, we didn't go out into the Haji land where Ali Baba could get a free shot at us, and we always had at least a sidearm, but there were a lot of things to see that were either in the Green Zone or in other areas controlled by the Coalition, and therefore relatively safe.

CHAPTER 65

Palaces and Playhouses

Saddam had a lot of palaces. Many of them were built with money that should have been going to help the Iraqi people, but since he was his favorite Iraqi person, I guess he figured that was okay. Probably the best-known of them was the Republican Palace, which was located right on the Tigris River in what became the Green Zone. Initially, it had four huge busts of Saddam, one on each corner of the roof. These things were enormous, each one being 4 meters (over 13 feet) tall. They were removed from the palace and it was turned into the US Embassy after the invasion. I was in there many times after it was the embassy, and the place still showed the opulence that Saddam demanded. The man was truly a megalomaniac who had statues and paintings of himself erected all over Iraq. The huge busts were moved to a small FOB just inside the Green Zone, so we made that another stop on our tour of the war zone. You never realized how big they were until you stood by one of them.

One of the other most notable palaces that we visited was the Victory Over America palace, which was located on Camp Slayer. When I wandered around in it, the place was abandoned and damaged by two hits from JDAM bombs. A JDAM (Joint Direct Attack Munition) is a GPS guided bomb that will hit whatever the pilot tells it to, even if he can't see the target, and they had flown these right into the building with devastating results. Saddam started building it after his "victory" over America in the 1991 Gulf War to free Kuwait. Not sure how he considered it a victory, but that's an example of how an inflated ego can warp reality. The place was still under construction when the war started, so it had never been finished. There were 12 military helmets set in an arc over the main entrance. Some sources said it was the helmets of defeated enemies, but I was told they were the helmets of his 12 favorite generals. Either way, it was just another example of his love for symbolism.

The place was huge. It was designed to have 75 bedrooms and the entire palace sat on the shore of a manmade lake. It was surreal walking around inside it. The grand ballroom on the main floor was literally the size of a football field. One of the oddest features was a smaller palace-like building built off to one side. The railings had cutouts shaped like hearts built into them. I was told by a local that it was to be called The Virgin House and that Saddam was planning to have young girls brought to live there who he would give to his favorite Ba'ath Party cronies for playthings when they pleased him. I have no idea if that was true or not, but given the other things he and his sons were known for, I wouldn't be surprised. True or not, it made me shiver to look at the place and think that it might have been true.

One of the most unique places we explored was what everyone called the Flintstones' village. Saddam had a thing for the Flintstones cartoon show and reportedly watched it with his grandchildren. At one point he built a palace-sized playhouse for his grandkids that looked like something out of the Flintstones TV show. As with all his other crazy construction projects, it was quite large. It had at least 20 rooms, a full kitchen, and even elevators to go between floors. It was right on the edge of a lake and had murals painted inside of it. By the time I explored it in 2005, the inevitable soldier graffiti was spray-painted all over it.

There were palaces on a lot of the Coalition military bases. Some of them were off-limits because they were being used as headquarters for one military unit or another. But many of them were just sitting there, empty and desolate monuments to one man's sick ambition. They were all replete with murals and frescos celebrating Saddam's greatness.

CHAPTER 66

Monuments and Museums

Everybody has seen pictures of the massive, crossed swords that stood on each end of the parade ground in Baghdad. As I've mentioned elsewhere in this book, I explored them and even crawled through the hot stuffy passage up into the hand that held one of them during my first week in Iraq. The arches, called the Swords of Qadisiyah, were built in 1989 to commemorate Iraq's victory over Iran. The hands were cast from Saddam's own hands and there were hundreds of helmets from dead Iranian soldiers around the bases of each one.

Just a little way from the parade ground was another, even more ostentatious monument, the Tomb of the Unknown Soldier. It also commemorates Iraq's victory over Iran and is designed to look like a Persian shield falling from the hand of a dying Iranian warrior. To us, it always looked like a big seashell that was falling over, but I guess we didn't understand the cultural symbolism. There's a museum inside the bottom of the monument that once contained war memorabilia. The lights didn't work when I was there, but the locals had looted everything out of it after the invasion anyway, so the place was just filled with empty display cases. On the other hand, the view of Baghdad from the top of the monument was excellent.

At one time the big square where all these monuments are was quite a cultural center. There is also another palace that once belonged to one of Saddam's sons-in-law. The story goes that he displeased Saddam at one point and fled into hiding. Saddam convinced him that all was forgiven and that he should come back home. Once he was back, Saddam's goons took him to the top of his palace and threw him off. It's very possible given everything else the guy did, but without researching it I can't say whether it's true or not.

Saddam liked to collect things. But where most people collect comic books and football cards, he went for bigger items. We spent an hour one day wandering around all the fighter jets he had sitting in a little park near the tomb. I'm guessing they were from the Iran–Iraq war too. His tank collection was more interesting to me since I had been an Armor officer when I was on active duty. It was stored up at the base in Taji. He had all sorts of tanks including a completely restored US Army Sherman tank from World War II. It even had "Hands across the water," the old slogan of the lend-lease program from back when the US was providing weapons to Britain during the war, painted on the hull. All in all, Iraq is a very interesting place. Too bad it isn't safe for tourism. It's still much too unstable and there are too many militias and terrorist organizations that have a political agenda. The United States and most other Western countries have "Do Not Travel" advisories in effect for it.

CHAPTER 67

Radwaniyah

Radwaniyah was a fascinating place. It is located just southwest of BIAP and is where Saddam's son Uday had his palace. If Saddam was a brutal dictator, Uday, and his brother Qusay, were little more than beasts. Uday was particularly vicious and was known to beat and rape young girls and murder his servants. His palace, known at the time simply as Uday House, was one of the few private residences hit in the US bombing campaign. Uday survived that, but he and his brother were eventually tracked down and killed by US troops while hiding in someone else's villa. By the time I got there, Radwaniyah Palace was being called the Crystal Palace by troops and contractors, and the palace and the large surrounding estate was the home of much of the special operations community working to capture the leaders of the terrorist campaign in Iraq.

It was difficult to gain access to the estate, but the client company employing me as a security contractor had a service contract for the area, so we were authorized to enter the base and would use that to gain access through the ECP so we could wander around and see the sights. We probably weren't really supposed to wander around all that much, but we figured we were obviously Americans with government-issued access badges, so if we ended up somewhere we shouldn't be, we could just say we were there on our client's business and got lost. Being prior military and security contractors, we knew they were pretty serious about security, but with so many different groups and organizations doing their own thing, it was hard to keep track of everyone.

On one occasion, several of the C-Suite executives from our employer came to Iraq to see the projects and ensure that the many contractors working for them knew they cared about the job they were doing. Mostly, they probably came for a lark, and to be able to tell their friends they had been to Iraq. Since they had a service contract for Radwaniyah, we were able to get permission for them to tour the base with certain provisions to satisfy the need to maintain secrecy and security.

As I mentioned, Radwaniyah was where a lot of special operations types worked out of. Folks like the SEALS and Operational Detachment Delta operators who went out in the dark of the night to drag terrorists out of their beds and safe houses. Understandably, these guys didn't want their pictures scattered around people's Facebook pages for the world to see, and I never took any photos there. One of the visiting VIPs, a vice president of something or other, didn't quite understand that.

I and the visiting executives had loaded up on a small bus for the tour, and as we stopped to look at something, a small team of military guys in three HUMVEEs were stopped on the other side of the bus. They looked like they were getting ready to head outside the wire. You could tell they weren't your average patrol by the way they were dressed and equipped. The lead HUMVEE had a minigun on the roof whereas most other HUMVEEs had a regular machine gun. One of the visiting executives started to "ooh and aah," and raised his camera for some pictures. Several of us quickly told him not to do that, but it was too late. One of the operators in the gunner position on the lead HUMVEE had seen him.

The guy bailed off the HUMVEE, boarded the bus, went straight to the visiting VIP, and demanded his camera. He started scrolling through the pictures, deleting them as he went. Satisfied, he handed the camera back to the would-be photographer, told him not to take any more pictures, and got off the bus. The guy looked around at us with a shocked look on his face. I just looked at him with a smile, raised my eyebrows, and shrugged. What else was there to say?

Unfortunately, committing faux pas wasn't limited to visiting VIPs. One day, one of the other security contractors and I decided to spend one of our down days riding around. We took one of the armored Ford Excursions and ran around checking out the little Haji shops around the bases that sold junk and bootlegged DVDs. On a wild whim, we decided to see what there was to see on Radwaniyah. We looked pretty official with our US government CAC badges and an armored SUV, so we told the gate guard we needed to check on something for our client, and after a few minutes and a call to his superior, he waved us through.

We drove around Uday's former estate just looking at everything. It was all pretty mundane, but the excitement of being someplace not many people had access to was a cheap thrill. As we turned down a road that ran through several rifle ranges, we got the bright idea to turn into one of them to see what it looked like. We drove around the side of the berm and stopped dead. There, spread out on the flat level ground were at least 50 Iraqis. They were all lying on their stomachs with hoods over their heads and their hands zip-tied behind their backs. Heavily armed American troops were walking around among them. These were obviously some of those guys the special operations boys snagged up at night.

We looked at each other and burst into laughter like a couple of school kids who just realized they were somewhere they weren't supposed to be. Fortunately, no one was paying any attention to us, probably deciding that if we were on the compound, we were authorized to be there. The guy with me had a beard, so for all they knew we were a couple of operators or civilian secret squirrel types. We quickly decided we should probably leave, so keeping it casual, we turned around and left, not stopping until we were back off Radwaniyah altogether. We were probably lucky no one bothered to come over and see who we were. I doubt the guys guarding those prisoners would have thought us being there was as funny as we did.

Locals

 I got to know a lot of Iraqis while I was there, some through working with them and others on a more personal level. Some guys ended up with Iraqi girlfriends, and at least one guy I knew married his and brought her back to the States. But that never appealed to me, and I got to know them in different ways. The Iraqis I worked with or around presented some interesting experiences and challenges. The ones I got to know personally were gracious and pleasant people. Either way, it was a different kind of experience than I would have had if I'd been there in the military where the uniform would have created a social barrier between me and them.

 I found that a little courtesy went a long way. That lesson was brought home to me through a small but, to me, significant incident. There were little shops selling bootlegged DVDs all over the bases and surrounding areas. You could buy any movie you've ever heard of for a dollar, so I would frequent them for DVDs to watch on my laptop in my downtime. As I walked into one of the larger shops one day, I noticed the owner sitting there with his kids. All the other contractors and soldiers coming into the shop walked past him as if he didn't exist. They weren't being rude, that's just the way Americans are. I noticed that he didn't look very happy, so as I walked past where he was sitting, I put my hand on my heart and nodded a greeting to him in the Arabic style of showing respect. His face lit up as if I had thrown him a $100 bill. When I went to pay for my DVDs, he grinned and told me that since I had shown such courtesy to him, all the DVDs I was buying were free. I was surprised and pleased by just how much a small thing like a respectful greeting made his day. How many times has someone done that in the United States?

 At one time, Iraq was an oil-rich nation with plenty of money. Like so many dictators, Saddam put more effort into aggrandizing himself than into helping his people. He reportedly had around 85 palaces and villas around the country. I saw maybe 20 of them myself and was inside quite a few. They were extravagant and built to glorify himself. By contrast, most of the Iraqi people were either poor or lived well below what Americans are used to.

It was also a very different society than Americans are used to. Although a relatively modern country, Iraq still had much of the tribal culture the Arab world is known for. In that culture, tribal bonds were more powerful than any identity Iraq has as a nation. Likewise, Islamic law carried more force than the law of the land. This meant that things that perhaps made little sense to Americans, were the way things were done there.

The main reason for these variations is that Iraq is an artificial country with boundaries imposed by the British after World War I. Up until then, the region had been controlled by the Ottoman Empire, but after their defeat in World War I, Britain defined the national boundaries and imposed a Hashemite monarchy which put the Sunnis in charge. They gave no consideration to the fact the Sunnis were a minority and that the Shia and Kurds hated them. The only thing that held Iraq together during the 20th century was the strong-arm leadership of its kings and later, dictator. When the US overthrew Saddam, the various factions were free to exercise their own cultural imperatives and fight their own battles of ethnic and religious differences. That's the way things stood when I got there in 2004.

CHAPTER 68

The Case Against Making Threats

Most of the companies subcontracting for security services were reconstruction contractors with projects to build everything from schools to water treatment plants all over the country. They provided engineering and construction management supervision, but the actual work was done by Iraqi and other construction companies from around the Gulf region. The reconstruction contractors were responsible for ensuring the work was done properly and on schedule.

However, some of our client's project sites were in areas that were so nonpermissive that it wasn't even safe for Westerners to go there with PSD teams. In cases like that they had to hire Iraqi construction professionals to oversee the work and check on the progress. They would issue the Iraqis cameras and have them go to the site every week to check on progress and bring back reports supported by photos of the work being done. Most of the Iraqis did their jobs, but there were always a few who tried to get over and falsified their reports to make it seem like they were going to the job sites when they really weren't. In one case, the local was only going to the job site about once a month while spreading out the pictures he took to make it seem like he was going every week. Unfortunately for him, he failed to take into consideration that digital photos have a time stamp showing the date they were taken. He eventually got caught and that's where we came in.

He was told by email to come to the camp and turn in all his equipment and records for the project. To get him to show up, he was informed his final paycheck would be held until he came in. He didn't have any choice, so he showed up, but once he got there, he began to argue about losing his job. He finally threatened that if he didn't get to keep his job, he would turn all the information about the project over to the insurgents, including the names of the company's local employees. That was when the Human Resources people called for security to come and talk to him.

I and another American security guy went to the HR office. We brought one of our Angolan guards with us—a big one. He brought his AK with him. We told the Iraqi that if he gave any information to the insurgents we would come and find him. In fact, we added, if anything happened to anyone associated with the project he had been working on, we would come find him. Better yet, we would send the big Angolan after him. As we said that, the Iraqi looked at the Angolan guard, who was a veteran of the South African-Angolan Border War. The guard looked back at him and flashed a perfect evil villain grin.

You really can't appreciate the kind of impact this had if you weren't there. It was almost as if we had rehearsed it. That Angolan guard was the epitome of an African warrior. He was a big handsome man with huge biceps and the blackest skin you can imagine. He was wearing sunglasses and when he smiled at the Iraqi troublemaker, all you could see was teeth. The guy was perfect, and he played his part flawlessly. If we had been making a movie and needed somebody to play a badass African mercenary, casting couldn't possibly have found anyone better.

I'd never imagined that an Iraqi could go pale, but that Iraqi did. His entire demeanor changed, and he suddenly became very contrite and cooperative. We had the Angolan and a few other security guys bundle him into a Suburban, take him just outside the Green Zone checkpoint, and drop him off on a street corner. We never heard from the guy again and nothing bad happened to any of the project team.

CHAPTER 69

Poverty

We hear about poverty in America, see it in the news, and there are, unfortunately, Americans who live below the American poverty standard. But most Americans don't know real abject poverty firsthand. In Iraq, I saw it. I mean living in a shack, scraping just to have food, that sort of hardship. Despite how wealthy Saddam and his government cronies were, and how many palaces he had, most of Saddam's people lived in poverty.

True, the Bedouins live in the desert the way they did hundreds of years ago by choice. The main difference now is that they have an old truck to haul their low tents around instead of using camels. They still have their herds of camels and goats just like they always have. It was a common sight to see their tents a few hundred meters off the road in central and southern Iraq. Their kids would stand by the road and beg us to throw them MREs and candy when we would go by with a slow convoy.

They were very dirty, but when you live in the desert water is too precious to waste just for washing. But they lived that lifestyle by choice because they had been doing it for generations. One Iraqi man I spoke to told us we had turned his country into a nation of beggars. Before Americans came to Iraq, the children would never dream of standing by the road and begging for handouts. The people were too proud.

The poor Iraqis in the cities didn't live the way they did by choice. There's a huge garbage dump on the side of Route 1 heading north out of Baghdad. When I say huge, I mean it must have covered hundreds of acres. I was surprised to see people living there in makeshift shacks and the backs of old trucks. The people run herds of goats through the trash so they can graze on garbage. I can't imagine an existence so bereft of hope that you would be satisfied living like that, but it had clearly been there for a very long time and was not something created by the war. There was a whole class of the population that lived that way.

I saw a different situation that *was* created by the war in the Green Zone. It was a theater that had once been pretty grand. Not a movie theater, but a genuine theater with a stage indoors and an outside amphitheater. There were several outbuildings, and it had become the home of roughly 30 families. I ran across it when a couple of us were exploring the Green Zone to see what was left of Saddam's luxurious monuments to himself. The main theater had taken a bomb that had gone through the roof and the stage, leaving a gaping crater below. The crater was full of garbage and human waste.

As we looked around, we noticed families and children playing around the ruins. They were cooking over open fires and drawing water in buckets and tin cans from a canal that ran behind the amphitheater. I later checked with the Air Force engineers who were handling the infrastructure of the Green Zone, and they said the canal was contaminated and carried meningitis. All told, about 30 families lived there. It was a grim situation. I decided I had to do something.

I got ahold of a church group back in the US and arranged with them to do a clothing and necessities drive to get some things for the people living in the theater. They really came through, and, in a few weeks, several boxes of clothes, toys, and hygiene items like toothbrushes and soap arrived. We had a lot more freedom of movement as security contractors, so I and another security guy loaded it all into an SUV and took it to the theater. I knew an interpreter whose family lived in a shack at the edge of the theater who tried to help me keep some semblance of order when I handed things out. I had completely underestimated the level of desperation these people were experiencing.

Trying to keep any order when distributing the supplies was hopeless. The people were so desperate that they practically stormed the vehicle. We ended up just setting the stuff out and letting them fight over it. And fight they did. I don't mean crowding and shoving; I mean fistfights between adults and children. But they gathered up every single item we were handing out, the winners walking away with bloody noses and big smiles. I recall one girl in particular, maybe 11 or 12 years old, who got a pair of blue pajamas. Every time I checked on the people at the theater after that, she would be running around wearing those pajamas as clothes.

I wished there was more that I could do, but I'd done everything I could. At least the people there had shelter in the abandoned buildings, but that's about all they had. The situation never changed in all the time I was around. As far as I know, they could all still be living there.

CHAPTER 70

Sunnis and Shīʿites

Our client had some projects up near Mosul, in the northern part of the country. It was a non-permissive environment, so they had a couple of Iraqi engineers who were keeping an eye on the progress of the construction of some schools and police stations. They would drive up and take pictures of the construction site, then drive back to Baghdad and prepare a report. I received a phone call one day asking me to come to one of the offices in the compound to meet with them.

When I got there, the two Iraqis were sitting in a conference room. They told me a story of being abducted on the road back to Baghdad. Insurgents, terrorists really, had set up a roadblock across the highway and were stopping every vehicle coming through, both cars and buses. They had well over 100 people sitting in a group in the dirt a little way off the road. They went around asking everyone for their names and any identification papers they had,

Most Iraqis are either Sunni or Shīʿite, not counting the Yazidi and Kurds up north. Most Americans think that is sort of like Baptists and Catholics, but the distinction is much greater. Shia and Sunni are two branches of Islam that abhor each other. The split has to do with the line of succession after Muhammad died without an heir in 632 AD. Sunnis thought the new prophet should be elected by Muslims, and Shīʿites believed it should be a succession to Mohamad's son-in-law Ali bin Abu Talib. The two groups can often tell each other apart by their names and where they go to the mosque. For example, Ali is a Shia name, and Sunnis would recognize it as such.

The people who set up the roadblock were Sunni, so they separated all the Sunnis from the Shīʿites. There were around 35 Sunnis, including the two guys working for my client. The terrorists told them they could leave because they were Sunni. The guys said that as they were going back to their car, they heard a lot of gunfire from back where the other prisoners were still sitting.

They were both shaken, but glad to be alive. If the people stopping the cars had been Shīʿite, it would have been them lying there bleeding in the dirt, and the Shīʿite prisoners going free. For our part, other than report it to the military, who may have reported it to whatever Iraqi government existed at the moment, there was nothing we could do. It was just another nasty event in a nasty situation. Most Iraqis were Shīʿites, but Saddam and his cronies had been Sunnis. For them, the war was still going on and both Westerners and Shīʿites were the enemy.

CHAPTER 71

A Sunni in Shīʿite Country

The hatred and animosity between Shīʿites and Sunnis don't just go one way. Southern Iraq is exclusively Shīʿite. The Sunni population is concentrated around central Iraq and Baghdad. Because Saddam was Sunni, he was very hard on the Shīʿites in southern Iraq, and it is common knowledge that the Shīʿites there have almost a pathological hatred of Sunnis. This makes it all the more amazing that one of my client's local subcontractors headquartered in Baghdad would send a Sunni to Nasiriyah, but that is exactly what happened.

Perhaps surprisingly, Iraq has excellent engineering professionals. My client was working with an Iraqi engineering firm from the Baghdad area and needed an engineer sent down to the project. So, they assigned one, who loaded up into a van and headed down to Nasiriyah. His arrival didn't go quite the way he expected.

He got almost to the main entrance of the project site when his vehicle was stopped by some locals. After a few minutes of conversation, they recognized him as a Sunni and dragged him out of his van. They beat him in the middle of the road until some of the guards were able to get them to back off. The locals shouted that they knew who he was and that if he didn't leave right away, they would kill him. The guy was given some immediate medical attention, after which he got back in his van and left to go back to Baghdad.

I was in Nasiriyah at the time, and I contacted my security counterparts at the client's headquarters in Baghdad and filled them in. I suggested they go to the subcontractor and ask them what they were thinking when they sent the poor guy to Nasiriyah. He was lucky to survive. In addition to his immediate well-being, we didn't need the negative PR of being seen as bringing Sunnis to the area.

CHAPTER 72

Street Kids

Street kids are a great source of information. They go everywhere and see everything, but no one pays much attention to them. There were a lot of kids running around the streets in Baghdad, both in and out of the Green Zone, and I cultivated a friendly relationship with many of them. Most of them were from poor families, so some treats or a few dollars went a long way to making friends with them.

And it paid off. They frequently filled me in on things they had seen and heard. Things like threats being made, people stealing things, and people sneaking things into the Green Zone. Most of the time it involved Iraqis doing things to Iraqis that wouldn't have any impact on us. But there were other times they passed on some good information.

In one case, some of them brought me hard copies of emails in English printed out by the American advisors from the International Police Liaison Organization (IPLO) working with the Iraqi police at the station down the road. I'll never understand why they printed out hard copies of official emails, and how they somehow ended up in a pile of trash on the street. But they did, and the kids brought them to me. I have to admit it was kind of fun going down to their office, asking for one of the IPLO guys by the name right off the email, and bringing his attention to his personal lapse in operational security. Considering some of the alternative situations that could have resulted from their lapse, a little embarrassment was pretty minor. It was also fun to inflict on a fellow contractor, what can I say?

CHAPTER 73

Alia and Ali

Two of the kids I met were a sister and brother named Alia (pronounced A-li'-a) and Ali. Alia looked like she was around 10 or 11 and Ali was younger by a couple of years. Ali didn't speak much English, but Alia was a very smart kid and spoke fairly good English, although she swore a lot. I asked her where she learned English and she said from the Marines, which explained plenty.

They lived with their mother, Sohad, in a mud-brick shack a little way from our compound. Their father was dead, and they barely eked by day by day. Alia didn't know when she was born. Sohad wasn't sure either, but she eventually found a government document with Alia's birth date on it. I was shocked to find out the skinny little kid was 14. I guess that's what a poor diet does to you.

A couple of us pooled money to help the family out from time to time. Things like getting their roof repaired and helping Sohad buy a washing machine. They were the lowest facet of Iraqi society, and they struggled every day. But unlike the people living in the abandoned theater, at least they had a place to live. How low their social status was, was brought home to me by an experience I had involving Alia and Ali one day.

I had been tasked with going to the helicopter landing field across from the Green Zone PX to pick up an Iraqi engineer who was being brought in to consult on one of the client's construction projects. Since it was inside the wire, I just took my SUV and went alone to meet his flight and bring him back to the compound. After picking him up, I was coming down Haifa Street where it ran through the Green Zone past Ibn Sina Hospital, when I noticed that the US Air Force security guys had Alia and Ali stopped and were talking to them on the sidewalk. It didn't look like a friendly conversation.

I pulled over to find out what was up. Alia said they were just selling gum, something they did a lot to get extra money, but the airman said they shouldn't be wandering around where they were by themselves. I told him that I knew them and knew where they lived, and that I would take them home. He was okay with that, so I told them to get in the back seat of my vehicle. The Iraqi engineer was offended. He immediately went into a rant that they were beneath him and shouldn't be allowed in the same car with him. He used some derogatory Arabic term for them that I didn't quite catch, but I'm sure it wasn't nice. I looked at him and quietly said if he didn't like it, I would let him out and he could walk. He shut up after that, and I dropped the kids off near their home and then took him to the meeting.

That was in 2006. I went back to Iraq on an assignment in 2010. While I was there, I looked up Alia and her family. They were still living in the same little house, but the back room had been destroyed by a rocket that insurgents had randomly fired into what was then called the International Zone. She was 18 years old then, and she excitedly told me that an American soldier was going to take her back to the United States and marry her. I told her that was great and spent about an hour with them before getting back to my assignment. I don't know what ever happened to them, but I have a feeling the soldier never brought her to America.

CHAPTER 74

Litigation Iraqi Style

I've mentioned the chaos that is Iraqi traffic elsewhere in this book, but it bears repeating. There is no rhyme or reason to Iraqi drivers or pedestrians. Everyone just goes wherever they want to when they want to, so accidents are inevitable. One such accident occurred just outside the gate to the pump station site while I was assigned there.

A young local pedestrian, a guy in his early 20s, stepped out in front of a truck and was killed. Other than the truck belonging to one of our Iraqi subcontractors, the incident had nothing to do with us. At least that's what we initially thought, but circumstances would prove that assumption to be mistaken.

In the United States when someone is injured or killed in a traffic accident, there is an insurance payout. If there was negligence involved there can be citations or possibly more serious charges. There is also a possibility of litigation if one party decides to sue the other.

Things don't work that way in Iraq. For one thing, there isn't much police involvement, especially out in the hinterlands where we were. For another, I'm not even sure people have auto insurance in Iraq. In this case, the family of the victim involved invoked a concept from the Qur'ān called *diyāt*. *Diyāt* is the paying of blood money to the family of the victim and is the alternative to *qisas*, which is retaliation. Essentially, it is like the practice of wergild common in medieval Europe, and I suppose not that much different from a wrongful death settlement, just without the lawyers.

Even though we were not directly involved in the accident, the family of the young man who was killed came to us. They held us responsible because the subcontractor's truck would not have been there at all if we did not have the construction project going. That seemed a little far-fetched to me, but by then I had learned not to try to apply Western reasoning to anything that happened in Iraq. They insisted on a settlement, or they threatened they would retaliate in some manner. Something we would rather avoid happening.

We got ahold of the subcontractor and had them send a representative to meet with us and the family of the victim. It took the usual haggling typical of arriving at any kind of agreement in Iraq, but eventually, the subcontractor agreed to a small payout. The family was not satisfied with the offer, but rather than drag the whole thing out, we offered to match the amount the subcontractor offered. That seemed to satisfy them, and we made sure the subcontractor paid their share if they wanted to keep their contract with the client. Sometimes security is more than just a bunch of guys with guns.

CHAPTER 75

Ibrahim and the City of Ur

Ur was an ancient city in what was once the region of Sumer in southern Mesopotamia, now part of Iraq. It was founded around 3,800 BC and abandoned around 500 BC after the Euphrates River changed course leaving the city high and dry. Some believe it to be the city of Ur Kasdim, mentioned in the Book of Genesis as the birthplace of Abraham, the patriarch of both Hebrew and Muslim religions. It is an amazing expanse of ruins, and I spent many of my off hours there exploring the ruins and tombs when I was assigned at Tallil AFB, both alone and with other contractors.

Through an unlikely set of circumstances, I was able to get to know one of the guides who, in happier days, took tourists and archeologists through the ancient city. When I was back in the US on an R&R period, I met a guy who had worked as a contractor at Tallil. He told me he and a couple of other Americans had put up the money to get an old man who lived near the base flown into Jordan for a medical procedure he required. The man's adult son, a professional guide who lived on the edge of the City of Ur, had been very grateful and the contractor said that if I went to see him and dropped their name the guy would probably treat me like royalty. The son's name was Ibrahim, the Arabic rendition of Abraham, which seemed fitting considering where he lived.

I found the ruins out in the desert and wandered around alone for some time before going to look up Ibrahim. He lived in a little mud brick house about a mile from the ruins. I went to the house I thought was the right one and knocked on the door. An Iraqi man answered it with a smile but looked a little confused. I told him who I was looking for and who had told me to look him up. As soon as I mentioned the other contractor's name, his face lit up in a grin and I was officially a member of the family. I visited Ibrahim and his family several times. Gift-giving is an important part of Arabic Islamic culture.

I would bring gifts for his children, and he would give me very welcome gifts of fresh fruit. The juicy, sweet watermelons were especially good.

At one point I asked if he would guide a group of us on a tour through Ur, and he happily said he would. I got around eight contractors together, and Ibraham gave us an amazing tour. His father had been a guide before him and had guided some archeological digs back in the 1960s. He showed us things we would have never found on our own, taking us down into some of the tombs and showing us the cuneiform writing hidden in hard-to-reach places where the builders of the tombs had signed their names 5,000 years ago. We collected around $400 for him for taking us on the tour. Since the war had stopped the tourist trade, the money meant a lot to him, and it showed on his face.

I've always been interested in ancient civilizations, and exploring the City of Ur was something I'll never forget. Sometimes I would go there alone and just sit in the ruins for an hour or two, imagining life 5,000 years ago. I've climbed to the top of the restored Ziggurat of Ur and looked into what archologists called the Great Death Pit, where a queen was buried along with six armed guards and 68 serving women, I went to Iraq because I wanted to go to war, but I gained a lot more from the experience than I ever imagined I would.

CHAPTER 76

Working with Local Sheiks

Sometimes, it is better to improve security by winning the hearts and minds of the locals than through brute force. Most Americans don't understand what a tribal culture much of the Middle East and Asia still has. It's more pronounced in more primitive places like most of Afghanistan, but it is still strong even in more developed countries like Iraq. We found that we could take advantage of that tribal nature to get the locals to help us secure key locations and infrastructure.

The power plant in Nasiriyah was a good example. It fell within the territory controlled by a local tribe and was, therefore, protected by that particular sheik. By meeting with him and showing the proper respect for his traditional leadership position, we could develop a mutually beneficial arrangement to keep the site safe. In this case, we offered benefits to his community like the client building a school, repairing some roads, and providing some wheelchairs for people from his villages who had been injured in the war.

In return, the sheik assigned his grandson and a cadre of fighters to protect the area around the power plant. The deal was sweetened by the fact that there was a man camp (basically a living area with trailers and a kitchen) adjacent to the plant that had been abandoned by the contractor who had the contract for the plant before our client. Typical of the way things were done on government contracts in Iraq, the previous contractor had left everything sitting there when they left. Multiple housing units looked like the occupant had just left to go to work for the day. Everything was intact. That included a well-stocked food storeroom. The grandson and his fighters called it Allah's Blessing because there was a lot of food there for them to enjoy. It was a win-win situation because once the sheik accepted the plant as being under his tribe's protection, it became a matter of pride and honor for them to defend it. None of us had to put ourselves at risk, and it increased his prestige.

I found that the best way to really understand the local culture was to immerse myself in it to the greatest extent practical, while still being relatively safe. This isn't an easy process, and it is especially difficult for the military because they are easily recognizable in their uniforms and are seen as something that is a danger to be avoided or distrusted. It was easier for us as civilians to make friends and gain the trust of the locals. But beyond that, it enhanced my experience in Iraq and everywhere I've worked since, both professionally and personally.

Iraqi Insecurity Forces

Being a security contractor in Iraq means you will inevitably have a lot of contact with both the US and Coalition military, and the Iraqi security forces, a generic name for the Iraqi police, military, and other various people who are legally armed and wearing some semblance of a uniform. This was especially true when I was doing convoy security.

There were US Army troops at the ECPs at all the bases we went to, and Army troops were out patrolling the roads as well as occasionally accompanying us on high-risk convoys. And, of course, the unfortunate US Marines who lived like trolls in bunkers for a week at a time under many of the major bridges along busy routes like Route Jackson, to prevent the insurgents from blowing them up or setting IEDs. We would always carry some extra cases of Red Bull and cans of Skoal to drop off to them. The Marines also ran the big warehouse at Abu Ghraib.

We had limited interactions with some other members of the Coalition. These included the British Army, who had responsibility for southern Iraq, and the Australians. The Italians had their own side of Tallil Air Force Base, but they weren't very active. Early in their deployment, one of their patrols was hit by an IED, and several men were killed so they never went outside the wire again. On the other hand, they had established several very nice restaurants on their side of the base. I guess everybody has their priorities, but I have to admit, the seafood marinara was excellent.

Then there were the Romanians. The Romanians were cool. They had a huge drawing of Vlad the Impaler (the historical inspiration for Dracula) on the T-wall around their camp, which said a lot about their outlook on life. They went out on the roads in their BTRs almost every day looking for a fight. A BTR is a Russian-designed eight-wheeled armored vehicle that may or may not stop the blast from an IED, but the Romanians didn't seem too worried about it.

But it was the Iraqis we dealt with most, whether I was doing PSD work, convoys, or site security management. Most interactions were relatively mundane. The usual moment of uncertainty as you approached the checkpoint or Iraqi government facility while they determined who you were, and we tried to determine if they really were Iraqi security forces or insurgents in disguise. They also had responsibility for security in the countryside surrounding most reconstruction sites. There were incidents over the time I was in Iraq where contractors were harassed and even abducted by Iraqis in security uniforms. In general, interactions with the Iraqis were initially a source of uncertainty that shifted into either aggravation or entertainment.

CHAPTER 77

A Force Divided

The most common group of Iraqi police we dealt with was the FPS, Facilities Protection Services. They were a poorly trained and equipped paramilitary force intended to provide static security for Iraqi government and construction sites. They were everywhere in their blue uniforms that looked like something a janitor would wear, usually armed with an AK and a single magazine. Because the Nasiriyah pumping station was owned by the Iraqi government, such as it was at the time, the perimeters were guarded by the FPS on one end, and the Iraqi 13th Infantry Division on the other.

The station was a 400-acre compound on the banks of the Euphrates River. It was designed to pump fresh water into the southern marshes to facilitate agriculture. Because it was so big, and because of Iraqi interservice contention, there was no coordination between the FPS and the Iraqi Army. Consequently, it fell to me to try to develop some sort of coherent defense plan.

The whole mess was complicated by the fact that southern Iraq was dominated by the Shī'ite Mahdi Militia. They didn't like Americans, but they didn't like the rival Iran-backed Badr Militia, and even factions within their own militia, even more. And none of them liked Sunnis. It was not uncommon to stand on the firing step around our camp within the NPS compound and watch tracers and RPGs fly back and forth between battling militia factions outside the wire. The FPS force assigned to the station was commanded by a police major (we'll call him Ali) who was a Madhi. His second in command was a captain who supported a rival militia. The unit was roughly split 50/50 between them. That may have been done deliberately to try to prevent either side from gaining too much power, or it may just have been a random mix. I have no idea.

We lived in a fortified camp within the station perimeter. One day I received a radio call from the Gurkhas manning the watchtower in our camp that overlooked the main gate asking me to come to the tower. When I got to the top, I looked out on a scene right out of a movie. The two factions of our FPS guard force were squared off facing each other in the area just inside the outer gate. They were armed with AKs and PKMs, all pointing at each other. They didn't look happy.

I told the guys in the tower to keep an eye on them and then radioed all of our security guys to instruct the engineers we were protecting to avoid the main gate until further notice. We expected it to devolve into violence, but they apparently got things straightened out because we never did hear a major firefight erupt, although there was some shooting on and off during the day. But that wasn't unusual in Iraq. Either way, we knew the FPS wouldn't be much use if we were attacked at any point since depending on who was attacking us, one half of them or the other could potentially side with the attackers.

CHAPTER 78

They Don't Let Me Torture People Anymore

The American reconstruction contractor who employed me at the pump station provided engineering and construction management services for the entire project. The actual work at the construction site was carried out by Iraqi and other regional construction companies using local labor. This was a big deal because southern Iraq was an extremely depressed area with unemployment hovering somewhere around 60–80 percent at the time, and the site employed 400 locals who needed the work.

This was a good thing because it made our security important to the locals. They didn't want to lose their jobs if we decided things were getting too hot and pulled out of the project. Unfortunately, because the locals were making a regular wage, it also supported a brisk criminal extortion business. Local tough guys would shake the laborers down for a percentage of their wages. In return, the locals received "protection" ensuring they would be healthy and available to work every day. Usually, it all happened after work hours outside the wire in the community, but one day one of the guys shaking down the local construction workers decided he would come into the site to harass some of the workers. I never did know what his name was, so I'll just call him Biker Guy because he rode one of the little motorbikes that were typical in Iraq.

Biker Guy was used to going wherever he pleased in the area, and he figured that applied to our site as well. He had no problem getting past the Iraqi FPS officers at the outer gate, which was just at the outer edge of the HESCOs. He probably knew some of them and either had deals with them or his reputation was nasty enough to intimidate them. Whatever the case, they let him in. Unfortunately for him, we maintained a second gate at the inner edge of the double HESCO barrier. It consisted of a heavy steel semaphore arm, a round pipe that swung up and down, and was manned by two of our Nepalese Gurkha static guards. A tower manned by two more Gurkhas with a machine gun overlooked the gate. If you've ever worked with Gurkhas, you know that they are incredibly loyal and will follow their orders to the letter. They also do not intimidate easily.

There was no way Biker Guy was ever going to intimidate them or talk his way past them. He blustered and threatened but the Gurkhas simply kept a calm, professional demeanor and told him no. When someone else who had the correct pass needed to get through, the guard opened the semaphore and let him through. Biker Guy tried to follow the other vehicle through on his motorbike. When the authorized vehicle was through, the guards quickly dropped the semaphore which caught Biker Guy at chest level, and swept him off his bike, which went a few feet into the site and then fell over in the weeds.

Needless to say, Biker Guy was pissed. He ranted and raged and eventually rode off on his motorbike, which the guards had helpfully retrieved for him from the side of the gate he was not allowed on. He vowed he was going to get his local militia buddies to attack the site.

I went to Major Ali, our FPS commander, and asked why he didn't do something about that guy. He looked at me with a straight face, and through the interpreter, told me that he used to be able to keep those kinds of guys under control, but since the Americans took over, he wasn't allowed to torture people anymore. I looked at him for a moment and then nodded before walking away. There wasn't much I could say to argue with that.

There was no attack, and we eventually gave Biker Guy some money to repair the damage to his motorbike, just to keep the peace. He never tried to get on the site again and was content to conduct his business outside the wire. But I couldn't help thinking that we Americans often make the mistake of thinking the rest of the world works the same way the United States does. It's an arrogant and uninformed outlook and has been the cause of numerous problems as we try to engage with people of other cultures. I would imagine now that we're gone, Major Ali has gone back to business as usual, and that might not be such a bad thing.

CHAPTER 79

Extortion and Police Commando Escorts

The Arab world has a concept called *baksheesh*. In simple terms, it means the same as bribery or greasing someone's palms to make something go smoothly. In the Western world, bribery is a negative thing and something to be avoided, or at least done secretly. Not so in the Arab world where it is normalized as a part of getting anything accomplished in life, hence the formal word for it. Everyone who has spent much professional time in the Middle East is familiar with *baksheesh* and has used it on occasion. I had a particular fixer I looked for whenever I flew out of the airport in Amman, Jordan. I would hand him $50, and he would save me a lot of time and hassle getting through security and to the boarding area by doling out a few dollars here and there to his contacts to smooth my way through. It worked out well for everyone and was just the normal method of getting by.

That's all well and good when it comes to getting through the airport line or finding a good deal on something, but it is less than desirable when it devolves into extortion and becomes a matter of life and death. Which is what happened to us in Nasiriyah.

When my employer first began the work on the project, the camp on the compound for the engineers and managers to live in hadn't been completed yet, so we lived on contractor's row at the edge of the Tallil Air Force Base, formerly the Iraqi Imam Ali Airbase. We had to travel back and forth from Tallil to the project site by PSD team. It was a terrible trip through numerous hostile Mahdi-controlled villages and down secluded and narrow roads through the marshes. Kids and adults in the villages frequently pelted our SUVs with rocks as we drove through and there were multiple checkpoints run by the local Mahdi militia to negotiate. Of course, retaliation was out of the question, so we just hunkered behind the armor in the windows and drove through. The trip could easily take an hour or more one way.

Shortly after we began making trips back and forth between the sites, our Coalition liaison officer came to see us. He was a British security contractor working for the Brits who had authority over southern Iraq. His job was to build a relationship with all the Iraqi police and military security forces and then be the go-between for them and reconstruction contractors like us.

He informed us that the Iraqi police strongly recommended we travel with a police escort on every trip to discourage attacks. We had our own intelligence resources in the community consisting of many local sheiks and businessmen who benefited from the work we were doing. Our sources assured us that we would not be attacked because we were providing 400 jobs that the economically depressed area desperately needed, so the people could feed their families. We told the liaison as much. Besides, we reasoned, how would a police escort prevent the team from being targeted by a command-detonated IED? Beyond that, we did not entirely trust the Iraqi police with detailed knowledge of our times and schedules for trips back and forth. The liaison went back to let the Iraqi police know we didn't feel we needed a police escort.

Three days later, on the next mission after our conversation with the police liaison, the team was attacked by an IED while traveling between Tallil and the project site. It was the first attack we had suffered. The PSD team consisted of three vehicles. The first and third vehicles were up-armored Suburban SUVs, and the middle vehicle was a factory-armored B6-level SUV. The team consisted of nine members, three in the first vehicle, two in the client vehicle, and four in the last vehicle. The IED targeted the passenger side of the first vehicle. The vehicle commander, riding on the passenger side in the front, was injured and eventually lost an eye. The trail Suburban and the client vehicle turned around and returned to Tallil while the rest of the team stayed at the scene of the attack to wait for recovery. An Army helicopter eventually arrived to medevac the wounded team member, and another team came out to recover the rest of the team and the disabled vehicle.

The missions did not follow any set schedule, and the only people notified in advance that there would be a mission were the police and the Coalition operations center. There had been no problems in the two months prior to the conversation about a police escort. Either the attack had been purely random and carried out by someone who just happened to be watching that road at that particular time, or someone who knew what route our convoy would be taking had set it up. The random theory gets thin because there were at least eight or ten other contractors located on the same contractor row we were in, and the route our team was traveling was not heavily traveled.

The only logical conclusion was that it was the Iraqi police who were behind the attack. They knew where our compound was and where the project site was. They knew we would be traveling between the two locations sometime that week. They even knew our general route, since there weren't that many ways to get around in the area. However, accusing them would be pointless since there would never be a way to prove anything and nothing would happen even if we could.

It would also make enemies of them, something we neither needed nor wanted. Beyond that, we were now in a position where we had no viable option except to agree to use their escorts. We still didn't trust them, now more than ever. But there was no question that the police were involved with the local militias, and if having them along on our runs back and forth was the only way to keep our teams and clients safe, we were left with no other choice.

The Iraqi police were more than happy to accommodate our request and assigned a unit of their elite police commandos as our regular escorts. Of course, operating funds were slim, and they would need us to contribute fees to cover the cost of fuel and vehicle use. This was also considered extra duty, so it would be nice if we could pitch in a little extra cash to the unit commander so that he could give each man in his team a little compensation as well. Needless to say, we agreed that we would be happy to do that. Major Hussein and his police commando team began accompanying us on our very next mission, and we never had another problem.

I have no idea how much we paid the police officially for each run since that wasn't my problem, but I know we regularly gave Major Hussein an extra hundred dollars personally after each trip. How much he passed on to each man in the team was up to him. After we had the camp set up at the project site, with a nice dining facility of our own, the police commando team frequently also had lunch there.

Baksheesh was alive and well, only this time it was extortion and a protection racket. But this was Iraq, and we had to play by their rules.

CHAPTER 80

Um Qasr Checkpoint

One of the tensest moments I had in Iraq was a face-off not with insurgents but with the Iraqi police. It was when I was doing convoy escort work, and we were on our way to the port of Um Qasr, just south of Basra in southern Iraq, almost on the Iraq-Kuwait border, to pick up our convoy. It was a big operation, and there were four of our four-truck teams involved. Basra had always maintained its independent attitude from the rest of Iraq. Even though the area was technically in the British Army AO, most of the security around the port was handled by the various Iraqi security forces and police.

We had already had one incident on the trip that left me sweating. We were the last truck, as usual, and a small British Army convoy had come up behind us. The first vehicle was a couple of Brits in a Land Rover Defender, essentially their version of an armored jeep. Since it wasn't an American HUMVEE, like the ones running around Baghdad and the rest of Iraq, my Kurdish tail gunner didn't recognize the Land Rover or the guys in it as a military vehicle. I heard him shouting and looked in my mirror to see that the Brits were right behind us. Before I could say anything, he fired a warning shot. I started yelling at him to stop, saying *"La, la, la!"*—the Arabic word for no—over and over. The Kurd in the seat behind me understood and joined me in yelling at the gunner. He stood down and I sat there sweating for a few heartbeats until the Land Rover pulled around us, followed by the short convoy of British vehicles. I radioed up to let the teams know they were going by.

I have no idea if the Brits realized he had fired a warning shot or not. Land Rover Defenders are armored and pretty tough, but no one likes to be shot at. They could have caused us some real trouble if they knew he'd fired a shot and decided to take issue with it. Maybe they did know and just didn't care. I'll never know, but it was definitely an "Oh, shit" moment and was on my mind later as we approached the Iraqi police checkpoint. I didn't need any more close calls. Unfortunately, that was exactly what I was about to get.

We were traveling with one of the other teams, but the other two teams had reached the city about an hour ahead of us. When we reached a big Iraqi checkpoint in the city, we could tell something was up. There were at least 20 angry-looking Iraqi police standing around with AKs. They were openly hostile toward us, which wasn't normal.

We only found out much later that they'd had an exchange of gunfire with another convoy escort team earlier that day. I have no idea what team or why. It had happened before we ever reached the city, but team vehicles and crews all looked alike to them, so they assumed we were the same guys.

We couldn't hear what was being said back where we were sitting in our up-armored trucks, but when the Iraqis began pointing guns at us, we figured something was very wrong. Each of our eight trucks had an American and three Kurds on board, plus one Lebanese interpreter in each team. Nobody can ever say that Kurds aren't always ready for a fight, and the Pesh quickly dismounted and pointed their AKs and RPKs back at the Iraqis. I got out of the cab with my M4 and got down in a firing position behind the open driver's door since it had at least some armor in it. I remember hearing "click, click, click, click" as the Kurds flipped the safeties on their rifles off, and thinking to myself, "Oh, this is gonna suck."

Fortunately, Casper and the Lebanese member from the other team waded into the situation with their usual fearless panache and sorted it all out, convincing the Iraqis that we were not the same people who had shot at them. After a few more intense heartbeats, everyone put their weapons back on safe, and we climbed back on the trucks. A few more minutes and we were on our way, glad to have gotten through it without shots being fired. We could have held our own, but even if we had come out on top, we would have been in a city filled with hostile Iraqis and probably British Army troops. Something that would not have ended well.

Checkpoints were a constant worry no matter who was manning them. Things could go wrong in a fraction of a second. When I was on a later contract, one of the client's project team members, a guy from the Netherlands, was shot by an Australian soldier at a checkpoint in the Green Zone. The kid had only been in Iraq for a couple of days, and it was his first shift on a checkpoint. Fortunately, the bullet only grazed the contractor's neck, and he survived.

The story of Giuliana Sgrena is another case in point. She was an Italian journalist who, with the journalists' usual naivety that they can go anywhere they want, went into Baghdad in 2005 to get a story, and was promptly kidnapped by terrorists. Italy eventually negotiated her release, and two Italian secret service agents picked her up and drove her to BIAP to leave the country.

They never arrived at the airport. Just before 9:00 pm, they were approaching a US checkpoint on the road to the airport traveling at a high rate of speed. No coordination had been made with the US military telling them she was on her way. The troops at the checkpoint challenged the car using hand and arm signals, flashing white lights, and firing warning shots in front of the car. When it didn't slow down, they opened fire. The idea is to hit the engine block and disable the car, but at night with the car approaching fast that's a lot to ask of even an expert marksman, let alone a young soldier. One Italian agent was killed, and Sgrena and the other agent were wounded. It was an unfortunate, but predictable, outcome of an unknown vehicle approaching a checkpoint at high speed at night in a war zone.

I can't blame anyone manning a checkpoint for being on edge. When you approach a checkpoint in a war zone, the guys at the checkpoint have a few seconds to decide who you are and what your intentions are. Our standard operating procedure (SOP) at night was to turn off the headlights, turn on the interior lights, and approach the checkpoint slowly. Along with the individual soldiers' rifles, there is usually a vehicle armed with a machine gun, often a .50 caliber that will go right through light armor. There really is no such thing as friendly fire.

CHAPTER 81

Goodbye to Nasiriyah

The pump station was a long-term project that stranded around 20 Western engineers and maybe 30 security contractors in a remote area in the Euphrates marshlands. It was also completely undefendable. The first thing I did when I took over the security for the project was to have our camp inside the project site hardened. More HESCOs, firing steps, and lots of sandbagged positions and barriers improved the camp, but it was apparent to anyone with any expertise that it could never hold out for long if insurgents or a local militia decided they wanted hostages. 2006 had been a very hot year for the insurgency in Iraq and things weren't getting any better.

I had developed contacts within the Coalition forces at Tallil and had assurances that they would try to send relief if needed. The Australians running the tactical operations center on the base had even provided me with one of their radios so I could make direct contact with them in an emergency. But we all knew it would take them at least two hours to reach us through the militia-controlled countryside, assuming they could get there at all. Our employer agreed with my assessment that the site was indefensible, and the project team was at serious risk if anything went wrong. The expats on the site had worked incredibly hard to get the plant going, but, out of concern for the safety of the contractors working and living on the site, the contractor made the difficult decision to turn the project back over to the Iraqi Ministry of Water in the early spring of 2007. It was time to get everyone off the site and back to the secure military base at Tallil.

But there was a problem. We had avoided major unpleasantness so far because the project provided some 400 jobs for the local economy. If we left, the local people would worry that those jobs might go away, so they would do everything they could to prevent that from happening. In their minds, if they could keep us from physically leaving the project, then they would go on working there.

We kept things very low-key as we prepared to shut the camp down. We didn't talk about it with anyone, and we didn't make a big deal about packing anything up. The plan was to load everyone up one morning and leave in one big convoy, so no one was left behind waiting for a second trip. That would protect everyone on the team by moving them all at once and eliminate the risk of having a second trip traveling over the same route on the same day.

Naturally, word began to get out, and the local construction contractors started asking questions. Our response was that the Iraqi Ministry of Water was taking the project over. No one would lose their jobs and the work would never stop. We had no idea if it would actually go that way ... probably not, but we weren't about to say that.

A few days before we were going to leave, my buddy Major Ali from the FPS came to see me. He told me he had orders not to allow our convoy to leave the site without a permit from the Iraqi governor's office in Nasiriyah. He said we would have to go there and get the permit in person. Of course, the area of the city where the governor's office was located was a no-go zone that was off-limits for all Americans. Since we were not allowed to go into the area where the governor's office was, we couldn't get a permit. Major Ali and whoever gave him his orders knew that.

It was time for a little *baksheesh*.

Major Ali knew what he wanted. He assured me that if I gave him a new computer and 10 American rifles, he could arrange for us to get out the gate to leave the project site. Theft, bribes, and corruption are such an everyday part of the Arab world that he found it hard to believe that an "important" man like me couldn't come up with the few items he was requesting, but I eventually convinced him I couldn't do that. Instead, I offered him a portable guard tower and two pallets of MREs. We were leaving them behind anyway, but he didn't have to know that.

He eventually agreed and we went on with getting everything ready to leave. When the morning came, we reassured all the locals that they wouldn't lose their jobs and that the work would go on without a break. We got everyone assigned to vehicles and their personal possessions loaded into a truck that would follow at the end of the convoy.

Just before it was time to go, I noticed our Pakistani cooks all standing around a minivan. They were wearing plate carriers and they all looked utterly forlorn. They were not our employees but worked for a regional contractor who provided dining facility (DFAC) services to hundreds of reconstruction contractors. When their employer was told we would be shutting down our camp, they told the cooks to just get in their van and drive back to wherever it was they were supposed to go.

The problem was that they didn't have permission from the Iraqis to leave the compound. They were also scared to death that they wouldn't get back through all the militia roadblocks alive on their own. Along with myself, we had over a dozen Nepalese static guards plus two PSD teams, having brought another one in for the move, giving us some 30 well-armed and trained shooters. They were just a bunch of unarmed TCNs in a van.

They didn't work for us, and we didn't have any authority over them or responsibility to protect them, but they had been good cooks and had fed us well, so we couldn't just leave them there. I told them to tuck their van in right behind the last vehicle in our convoy and not to stop for anything. As we began to pull out, I made eye contact with Major Ali and gave him a nod with my hand touching my chest over my heart in the traditional sign of respect in the Arabic world, which seemed to please him. We had the windows down, and I suddenly heard the guards start yelling for the Pakistanis in the van to stop. But to their credit, they just stared straight ahead and kept driving. The trip back went without serious issues, and they followed us all the way back to Tallil where they split off to go to their company's compound. A happy ending for everyone.

The other contractors and I spent the next week or so at our compound on the edge of Tallil AFB waiting for our flights home. For me, it would be more than just the end of this contract; it was time to go home. I had been in Iraq for 33 months, from August 2004 to April 2007. It had been a great run, but I was tired. I was ready for comfortable clothes, good food, and not having to look over my shoulder all the time.

Losses

Although most of the Iraq war was considered a low-intensity conflict, it still extracted a high price in human lives. People are generally aware that as of July 2021, 4,431 American troops had been killed by all causes, including combat and accidents, and another 31,994 wounded. That's a high cost in life and suffering among the American military.

What most people are not aware of is that by July of 2007, 182,000 contractors were working on US government-funded projects, 21,000 of whom were Americans, and another 43,000 were from other countries outside Iraq. Between March 2003 and June 2011, at least 1,487 contractors were killed and another 10,569 injured. One report stated that 53 percent of all fatalities in the first six months of 2010 were contractors.

Not all of them were Americans, and there were likely many deaths and injuries among some TCN groups that were never reported and thus not counted in that number. But no matter how you count it, contractors in Iraq were in a great deal of danger even if they weren't in combat or private security roles. A few of those killed and injured contractors were friends of mine. People I knew and worked with on a daily basis. During my time in Iraq, seven people that I knew well were killed, and at least 12 were seriously wounded. I recount some of their stories elsewhere in this book. Here are a few more.

CHAPTER 82

Archie Gets His Nose Shot Off

Archie was a former British Royal Marine. He had been one of the small force of Royal Marines on South Georgia Island for the Battle of Grytviken on April 3, 1982, when the Argentine Navy invaded the island during the Falklands War. He and 21 other Royal Marines had held the island against three times their number of Argentine Marines. They managed to kill three Argentines, shoot down an Argentine helicopter, and damage the Argentine Navy corvette ARA *Guerrico*, before being forced to surrender. In 2004 he was a security contractor in Iraq.

Archie's PSD team was making a run up Route 1 when the team came under fire. The insurgents were hidden along the side of the road and popped up to start shooting as the team went by. Everyone on the right side of the vehicle returned fire. Archie was next to the open window when a bullet came in and very neatly took his nose completely off. Archie was a hard dude, and he didn't miss a beat emptying his magazine toward the ambushers while the driver yelled for him to put pressure on his wound.

The team got to the nearest base so Archie could get immediate care, and then went to a bigger facility once they were back in Baghdad. Archie was back at camp that evening looking miserable. It was obvious he was in pain, so we just checked in on him and then left him alone. He left the next day and I never saw him again. The company told us they would cover all his expenses and his job would be waiting for him whenever he wanted to come back. As it turned out, the company bailed on everyone a couple of months later, so I doubt they kept their promises to Archie. I hope his short stint as a contractor was worth the suffering and permanent disfigurement he experienced.

CHAPTER 83

The Trials of Job

Job was one of the Americans working on the convoy security contract with me, although he was on another team. A former soldier, he was a Christian of strong beliefs and used the call sign Job. He said he'd chosen Job as his call sign because no matter how tough things got, he could look at the trials Job went through in the Bible and know he could handle it. He was a young man, somewhere in his late 20s, who had the look of a nice kid you might see working at an auto mechanic shop. He never made a big deal about his spiritual beliefs; they were just always there in his calm demeanor and constant smile.

Job's team was escorting a convoy somewhere on the outskirts of Baghdad when they came under fire from insurgents on a highway overpass and the roadside. They followed SOP and changed lanes under the overpass, but there were just too many insurgents shooting at the slow-moving convoy from above and from the sides of the road. Although the doors of the trucks we used for convoy escort had armored plates, the roofs of the cabs did not. Several AK rounds came through the roof into the cab. One of them hit Job in the side of the neck. In all the confusion of shooting back and trying to get out of the kill zone, he was dead before anyone could get to him. No one could even check on him until they were able to stop by the side of the road and set up a perimeter.

He was a good guy. Always happy and easy to be around, as most of the people I have known who had strong faith have been. He'd come through his time in the Army without a scratch. I never knew the reason he'd decided to come to Iraq, but whatever it was, he gave his life for it. In the Bible, God gave Job trials to test his faith. I believe the Job I knew passed his own test of faith and courage.

CHAPTER 84

Yam

Yam was Nepalese. He was on my team on my first PSD contract. He was one of the most dependable people I have ever known. Always friendly and quick with a smile, he was liked by everyone who knew him and always exchanged greetings with everyone as if they were an old friend. He was one of the guys in the other vehicle when the first IED of my Iraq experience went off on the road to Haditha Dam. I recall him shaking his head when we stopped and saying how lucky we had been that the IED hadn't caught us solidly when it was detonated.

After the company we worked for disintegrated, he was one of the Nepalis left high and dry when the owners skipped town. I ran into him several times for a few months after we went to different contracts. The Iraq security contractor community was like a small town, and you constantly saw people you used to work with or just knew in Iraq. I used to joke that I was more likely to run into someone I knew at the airport in Baghdad or Amman than in my hometown.

Yam's fate was related to me by someone else, actually by a couple of other people at different times. That means the story is either accurate or that I heard the version most frequently told, but it's all I have to go on. It goes like this.

Yam was working PSD with another company. While on a run his vehicle was disabled and crashed at high speed on the side of the highway. It was a bad crash, and, as was common with PSD teams, no one was wearing a seatbelt and some of the guys were thrown out of the vehicle. The other vehicle circled back to check on everyone but didn't find any signs of life on the people they could reach easily. The client's vehicle kept going to get the client to safety, which was also SOP. The other PSD vehicle took off to catch up with it and left the dead team members lying there to be recovered after the clients were safe.

When the recovery team arrived at the crash site, they could not find Yam's body among the dead team members. That could only mean that Yam was alive, or at least had been immediately after the crash. As the story goes, no one knew what happened to him, but since his body wasn't found, and he didn't surface at a hospital or military base over the next couple of days, it was determined that he had probably been captured by the insurgents. If that was the case, everyone figured that unless they released some kind of statement or video, no one would ever know where he was or if he was alive or dead.

The question was answered a few days later when Yam's body was dumped near a military checkpoint in Baghdad. He was dead, and it looked like he may have been tortured, although it was hard to tell. As near as anyone could figure out, Yam had survived the crash but been thrown far enough from the vehicle that the team didn't see him when they looked for survivors. The insurgents found him after the rest of the team left but before the recovery team arrived and took him prisoner. Given the atrocities like torture and beheading that the insurgents were carrying out on any foreigner they could capture, Yam probably had it pretty rough until he finally died, either from his injuries or by being murdered by his captors. So passed Yam.

I can't swear to the accuracy of the story. It is at least possible and plausible in light of some of the things that were happening in Iraq during that time, and probably still are. All I can say for sure is that I never saw Yam again or talked to anyone else who had seen him after the story circulated. I like to think that it isn't true, and Yam just went back to Nepal.

CHAPTER 85

The Cost of a Ringtone

Arturo (not his real name) was a Filipino contractor who ran a motor pool and logistics yard for a services contractor at what was then called Camp Victory adjacent to BIAP. We got to know him simply because the yard he ran was adjacent to the camp where I was stationed for a few months. Arturo was friendly, and it was obvious he was enjoying his job and time in Iraq. Like pretty much every other expat in Iraq, he bought one of the prepaid phones you could pick up at the airport or most of the little shops around. They were cheap little things that you put money on by buying cards and entering a code, but they worked fine even for international calls.

You could buy different ringtones for them, but they didn't have app stores, so to get it on the phone you had to go to a shop that sold phones and have it added on. Arturo wanted a new ringtone, so he called around Baghdad to find somewhere to get the one he wanted. He had an Egyptian coworker (I never knew his name) who helped him with the Arabic needed to talk to the shop owners. He found one in Baghdad, and since Camp Victory was at the end of Route Irish, it was only a short drive to go into the city. Short, but not safe.

Arturo told the shopkeeper he would be right there and persuaded his Egyptian friend to go with him to get the ringtone added to his phone. From what could be pieced together, the shopkeeper told the insurgents that two internationals would be coming to his store shortly because the insurgents were waiting when Arturo and his friend arrived. They shot Arturo in the head and left his body in the vehicle. They told the Egyptian that, since he was a Muslim, they wouldn't kill him, but he was to drive the vehicle with Arturo's body in it back to Camp Victory, and then he was to leave Iraq immediately.

When he reached the checkpoint to go onto Camp Victory he told his story to the soldiers. When we asked the new guy at the logistics yard where Arturo was, he told us the story. It was very easy to drive off the bases since there was no traffic control in that direction. After everything that had happened over the past months, it was surprising that Arturo took the risk of driving into town for a ringtone, but I guess he assumed everyone else was as nice a person as he was. Something that isn't safe to do anywhere, and certainly not in a conflict zone where a dirty guerrilla war is going on. It was a meaningless death that accomplished nothing for either side.

CHAPTER 86

A Tale of Three Contractors

In September 2004 an incident occurred that only involved us through proximity, but really brought home how critical it was to make good decisions in Iraq. It was heavily covered by the media and was one of the first well-publicized abductions and murders of Western contractors. Especially since their executions were posted online for everyone to see.

It involved three men who were working for a construction company in Iraq. Two, Jack Hensley and Eugene Armstrong, were Americans, and the third, Kenneth Bigley, was British. The men lived in a villa in the Mansour district, an upscale neighborhood where Western contractors paid as much as $25,000 monthly to rent a nice villa. Their villa, where the kidnapping took place, was three doors down the street from the villa my employer rented and where I stayed some nights.

The villa the three men lived in was not fortified and didn't have any special security modifications. They relied on some local Iraqi guards to keep them safe. By contrast, our villa was surrounded by 12-foot T-walls with RPG nets installed around the tops. We also had a force of local guards, and we were all armed as well, making it a reasonably hard target.

The night of the abduction, the contractor's guards did not show up for their shift. There was some indication that they told the men they had been threatened for guarding Westerners. The men knew their home was being watched and that they were in danger, but decided to spend the night in their villa anyway. I don't know how they traveled back and forth from the villa to their work sites. They may have had a PSD team that picked them up in the mornings, but we really didn't know. Nor were we aware of the drama that was playing out just down the street from us until the next day.

According to some local witnesses, the men were drug out of their villa at gunpoint at around 6:00 am. We had local staff working as cooks and housekeepers, and they talked to the neighbors and got the story for us. We were speechless with disbelief that these guys would just sit there defenseless and wait to be kidnapped when our well-protected villa was three doors down the street. Had they come to our door when their guards didn't show up, we would have taken them in without question.

A terrorist group run by the soon-to-be infamous Jordanian-born terrorist Abu Musab al-Zarqawi announced they had the men and would kill them if their demands were not met. They demanded the release of all female Iraqi prisoners the US and Britain were holding, even though both countries said they didn't have any female prisoners. The men were beheaded with videos of the murders posted on the internet for their families to see. The US located al-Zarqawi in Iraq a couple of years later and killed him by dropping a 500-pound bomb on the building where he was.

The abduction and murder of the three innocent men who were just there to make some money and rebuild Iraq affected us all, both because of their naive decision to stay in their house when they knew they were in danger, and because they were literally abducted while we slept a few hundred feet away. The neighborhood was known as a place where Western contractors lived and was the target of several attacks because of it. A few weeks later a car bomb detonated down the street and blew the windows out of our villa, but I was not there at the time. Other than some flying glass, no one was seriously injured.

The kidnapping and murder of Westerners affected all of us. We still did our jobs like we always did, but we all vowed never to be taken alive. In war, being a POW is rough, but you have a chance of making it home when the war is over. That isn't the case in the Middle East, especially not if you are captured or abducted by insurgents or terrorists. We were determined that our families would never have to watch a video of us being beheaded. It may sound extreme, or even a little melodramatic, but we all agreed to do whatever we had to not to be captured or let each other be taken. I kept a frag grenade in my vest just in case.

CHAPTER 87

Need a Little Help Here

The year 2006 saw a major increase in IED and VBIED attacks against both the military and contractors. Everybody, our teams included, was getting hit more often and more effectively. There was no such thing as a "routine" PSD run anymore. Attacks were sudden, happening so quickly that it was often difficult, or even impossible to recreate the moments before the attack to try to understand what had actually happened or how it could have been avoided ... if at all.

In an effort to figure out what had happened during an attack, some of the contractors began wearing helmet cams. A recording could be played back and slowed down to see if there had been any indicators of an impending attack that could be used to reduce the effects of future attacks. A video was also helpful if there were any disputes that arose from the actions of a team when they were out on the road and an incident occurred. One of those helmet cam recordings gave us an eerie opportunity to experience an attack that hit one of the other teams. An attack that took another life.

A South African team member, I'll call him Altus, was driving the lead up-armored Suburban of a three-vehicle PSD movement. Ruaan, the team member in the front passenger seat, had a helmet cam on his helmet. It was a local run, meaning it was from the Green Zone to somewhere in the Baghdad area. Most IED attacks happened in the morning. Ali Baba would sneak around in the night, hoping to set up his IEDs under the cover of darkness, and then set them off in the morning so he could get back to his safe house and get ready for the next night. Night patrols and aircraft with night vision capabilities would interdict some of them, but others would always get through.

It would have been nice to be able to avoid this morning IED rush hour effect, but since the clients usually needed several hours at a field site to get their work done, it was necessary to get an early start on the workday. Altus's team was making one of these runs when they were attacked by an IED. We gathered in the operations room to watch the helmet cam video later that day.

The camera was not pointing at Altus when the IED went off, so we just heard it and saw the video jerk around as the shock wave tossed Ruaan and the vehicle around. Altus was knocked unconscious immediately. Fortunately, his foot slipped off the accelerator pedal and the vehicle began slowing down. Ruaan was a highly experienced contractor, and he kept his cool. There was a lot of smoke and dust in the air, and we only caught a glimpse of Altus as Ruaan glanced over at him sitting slumped in the seat.

Then, the video swept to looking through the windshield as Ruaan tried to get control of the vehicle. The radio gear, GPS tracker, and panic button were mounted on the floor between the two front seats, which prevented Ruaan from getting his feet over to the driver's side so he could press the brake pedal. All he could do was reach over and steer the vehicle to keep it from running off the edge of the road. We could hear him on the video, his voice calm and in control, as he repeated, "Need a little help here," several times.

The procedure in a situation like that is for one of the other vehicles to speed up and get ahead of the vehicle that is out of control. Once it's ahead of the runaway, the other vehicle pulls in front of it and gradually slows down until it can match speed with the runaway to the point that it gently bumps against the rear bumper. Then the rescue vehicle gradually slows, bringing both vehicles to a stop. The video ended at that point as Ruaan took his helmet off and the team got Altus out of the vehicle and called for medical evacuation.

The Coalition had taken control of Ibn Sina Hospital in the Green Zone to treat wounded troops and contractors, and that's where Altus was taken. It was the most modern hospital in Iraq, and three of us were able to visit him in the trauma ward that evening. He looked bad. He was still unconscious, and his head had taken the brunt of the blast. One side of his head was pretty torn up and swollen to twice its normal size. His left eye was swollen shut.

The ward was a grim place. There were several occupied beds with unconscious patients in them. One was a young American soldier with half his leg gone; the others were in equally bad condition. I asked the medic on duty if Altus was going to lose his eye. The young man looked at me and very matter-of-factly said, "His eye is the least of his problems." At first, the words and his tone of voice seemed a little callous, but then I realized that he saw and dealt with this scene every day. He had no choice but to emotionally distance himself from it all if he wanted to maintain his sanity.

Altus died that night without ever regaining consciousness. I was able to get the Army to give us permission to use a small building they had designated as a chapel to hold a memorial service. We had the standard salute to a fallen soldier of his boots, rifle, and helmet at the front of the room. After the comments from his team members, a piper dressed in Highland garb marched in through the back entrance playing "Amazing Grace" on the bagpipes. I listened to the song being played on the pipes as I wrote this and could still see it vividly. I went to several memorials while I was in Iraq, but this one always stuck with me. I don't know why that contractor had brought his pipes with him to Iraq, but he got a lot of calls to use them. Too many.

CHAPTER 88

Body Armor Works

Body armor was mandatory for the clients when on a PSD run. Nobody had to tell us to wear it, but the clients hated it, complaining loudly about the weight and the heat. Some even went to the lengths of taking the plates out of their plate carriers and trying to sneak through that way. We eventually got to the point where we checked them before departing. We refused to move the vehicle until everyone was wearing armor. They never seemed to grasp that it could save their lives if/when something happened, but it would and did.

In one instance that would have added another chapter to this section on losses, an IED went off, targeting one of the other teams. The insurgents' timing was bad, so the only damage was some small holes from splinters in the vehicles. But one splinter about 3 inches long went into the passenger compartment and hit one of the team members. He didn't realize he'd been hit until he reached camp and exited the vehicle.

As was usual, we knew the attack had taken place and several of us were waiting when the team arrived to check on everyone and hear the details of the incident. When he got out of the SUV, he noticed that his jacket pulled to one side when he stood up straight. Looking down, he saw that the 3-inch-long steel splinter had nailed his jacket to the ceramic armor plate in his carrier. If not for the armor, it would have entered his body right around his large intestine with catastrophic results. Fortunately, the armor stopped it, and because it was a ceramic plate instead of a steel plate, we all saw it. If the plate had been steel, the splinter would have glanced off it, but since the plate was a ceramic composite, the splinter stuck in it like an arrow point. We took a picture of it and posted it where the clients usually gathered for the teams to pick them up.

The clients were also required to wear helmets in the vehicle and to fasten their seat belts. The helmets weren't to stop bullets or splinters, they were to protect the client's head if the vehicle was tossed around or rolled over during an attack. Likewise, the seat belts were to keep them from flying around inside the vehicle. A skull fracture was a definite possibility in a violent rollover or explosion.

The importance and effectiveness of the policies were demonstrated when one of the client's vehicles was targeted by an IED. The car bomb crossed the center divider and exploded next to the B6 armored Ford Excursion. The Excursion was totaled and ended up on its roof with the client hanging upside down in his seat belt. The team got him and the other team members out and away from the scene, Miraculously, they all only suffered minor injuries, although the client had permanent hearing loss. I wasn't on that mission but went to see the vehicle later. Refusing to wear your personal protective equipment because it is hot or uncomfortable could be a fatal decision.

Epilogue

After two and a half years, I left Iraq. I'd been there from August 2004 through April 2007. The environment had gone from the Wild West days immediately after the invasion to the more ordered and regulated period after the battles of 2006. The greatest threats had progressed from small arms ambushes at overpasses to roadside EFPs and VBIEDs that could take out an infantry fighting vehicle. I was tired and felt like I had been there through the best years and needed a little time back in the USA.

My mother passed away in February 2007 while I was assigned to the pumping station project out in the remote militia-infested marsh country. The logistics and risks of having a team take me out so I could try to get a flight out of Iraq to make it to her funeral were unrealistic. At best, if all went smoothly, and nothing ever went smoothly in Iraq, it would have taken me at least five or six days to get back to the United States. That would have been pushing it to make the funeral. Besides that, I didn't feel right asking people to risk their lives just so I could attend her funeral, so I didn't go. I'm sure she would have understood.

The shutting down of the project where I was the site security manager was the impetus for my departure. I had tried for months to arrange some kind of military quick reaction force that could come and support us quickly if we were under attack, but no one was willing or able to provide one. The Australians had promised to respond if we called for help, and I even had one of their radios for direct contact with their tactical operations center. But they would have to come by ground through numerous militia-controlled villages, and a lot of narrow dirt roads through the marshes. There was no way they could arrive in under two hours, assuming they got through at all.

We had asked the US and British Coalition forces if they would release helicopters to come if we needed them, and they flat-out said no. All this was going on at the same time the construction work on the project was hitting all sorts of difficulties. These were mainly due to the poor quality of the available materials and the skill level of the local workforce, which made them very difficult problems to overcome. The two situations combined to cause the client to declare a force majeure to their overall client, the DoD, and the project was turned over to the Iraqi Ministry of Water to complete. The bottom line for me was that my job no longer existed. I could have found another contract, but I decided I'd had enough of Iraq and went home.

I didn't stop working as an international security contractor. I continued to travel to harsh environments and conflict zones for another 13-plus years. I made another short trip to Iraq in 2010. My work also took me to Afghanistan several times, along with Pakistan, the Palestinian West Bank, Israel, Kenya, and Jordan among other places. I had many personally and professionally exciting and significant experiences. I oversaw the relief of my employer's three project teams in Haiti after the 2010 earthquake. I worked security for an airfield dedication in Afghanistan, attended by the US and British ambassadors. I was in Cairo during the 2011 Arab Spring revolution when Hosni Mubarak was overthrown.

But nothing had the personal impact that my time in Iraq did. I'd had my war. Not like a soldier, but in a far different and more personal way because I was there by choice. I'd worked with some great people and seen some of them killed and injured. I experienced some historic moments. I drove past the place where Saddam was being held many times and I remember the Iraqis driving through the streets cheering and blowing their car horns when he was convicted on November 5, 2006, and sentenced to death. I'd seen the best and the worst of humanity. As I wrote this book and reflected on the many events and incidents that had occurred, I was struck by just how chaotic being out on the road had been. We had always reported incidents through channels to the US military, but we never knew if they had even investigated them. There was just too much going on and too many incidents to ever find out. I'd tested myself against all the boogeymen that haunt our psyche. I'd known fear and overcome it, and for me, that was the most important thing. I had been shot at and my vehicle had been targeted by IEDs on more than one occasion, but the next day, I put my kit on and went back out on the road to do my job even though I was there by choice and could have gotten on an airplane home at any time. It was something I needed to do. I have always sought adventure and opportunities to test myself, but I will forever carry my time in Iraq in my heart and mind as one of the most profound experiences of my life.